"Matthew Fox's powerful book is not an abstraction. It is a window into a tragic reality: a thoughtful, feeling, powerful memorial of how wrongful convictions happen, and the consequences they wreak."

Professor David R. Dow, University Distinguished Professor at the University of Houston Law Center, Texas Innocence Network Founder. Author of "Executed on a Technicality;" "America's Prophets: How Judicial Activism Makes America Great;" and most recently, "The Autobiography of an Execution."

"Wayland Matthew Fox has tasted the "via negativa", the dark night of the soul, and emerged with something important to say. His poetry sheds light and insight into his soul journey through the wilderness of our justice system, and his stories are important to hear. It is scary how many people incarcerated do not have the means to be well represented. This narrative is his story, not of victimization but of authentic moral outrage. I highly recommend it."

Matthew Fox, Author of "Original Blessing," "The Hidden Spirituality of Men," "A Spirituality Named Compassion" and 24 others

"As a personal witness to Matthew's deplorable experience with our broken judicial system; his heartbreaking tale demonstrates the power of God's greatest gift; the power to choose. Matthew chooses to overcome, never to be beaten, to grow stronger; mentally and spiritually and to be committed to an ever present positive attitude; regardless of his horrific circumstances. He is a beacon of light. His attitude, love and perspective are a testament to us all. I would highly recommend this book to anyone facing seemingly insurmountable odds.

Terry Buske
V.P of National Sales, Optio Solutions, LLC.

"While the United States legal system may be among the best in the world, the fact is that it is fallible. Sometimes, miscarriages of justice occur and innocent defendants like Matthew Fox are convicted. Rarely, these defendants are able to win their freedom. Matthew Fox's book takes us behind the scenes and shows us firsthand, with the brutality of fact, the nightmare of being falsely accused. His unblinking testament should be read by anyone interested in the truth and justice."

Neal Davis
Neal Davis Law Firm, PLLC

"The writing is brisk and clear and you will feel like you are on a ride at the carnival of   horrors. This ride however is real, and is happening as we speak. Fox's deeply spiritual message is "WAKE UP", and if this chronicle doesn't awaken a new level of outrage in all of us, then the social prison of unconsciousness is wider and deeper than I ever imagined."

Robert K. Beare, Jr. MA, LPC
Psychotherapist
Author of "The Art of Being Alive"

"Matthew Fox's original narrative is a gut wrenching expose of the flaws in our legal system told from the perspective of the wrongfully convicted. Jurors don't seem to take their responsibility of a man's life seriously enough anymore and are somehow able to convict based on the testimony of one person against another without any physical evidence and without considering the credibility or motives of the one individual testifying.

Matthew's story is also one of resilience and determination fueled by spiritual faith. The way he uses his time in jail to help others and to see the good in people is truly remarkable."

Karen Cooper

"This is the story, sometimes gut-wrenching, sometimes poetic, sometimes in your face, told by Matthew Fox of his inferno experience resulting from being wrongly accused of sexually abusing a child. It is also a powerful image of what becomes a triumphant sub plot: one of hope, transformation and compassion, guided by his deepening Christian faith. He speaks with the visceral outrage that brings to life the wanton injustice and the inhuman horrors he experienced firsthand in the US criminal justice system. Be warned that his words are challenging and hard-hitting, as they are provocative and eye-opening."

Jerry Goodman, LCSW, CSAT

"I have been honored to know Wayland for over forty-five years. His narrative is powerful and evocative of horrors most of us will never know as well as the story of the transcendence of the human spirit. It is a call to awareness for all who forget that 'there but for the grace of God go I.' His experience is sadly shared by many who run afoul of the legal system in the United States. He has written a true story of the unseen and unheard among us."

Ann Perkins, Lifetime friend

"I can honestly say this is a most compelling book. How a society treats its people is a direct reflection of the nature of its soul. This is the story of a man who has "Walked his Talk" in the dungeons' of Houston, Texas."

Walt Stewart, Artist

"A heart-breaking, soul-trying account from a man who experienced our "justice" system. Reading it will pose a question: could I have come out of this with his strength of human spirit?"

Don Burton, A friend of 20 years

"What God has done here, is what God has always done; taken a person and turned him inside out. Remolded him, and then refocused him! He has revealed His heart in Matthew, and it is my prayer that this book lights a fire in all who read it to look at those so often overlooked. May God continue to humble us, save us, love us. May it be His hands that pull up our broken systems and set them right! May it be His same heart that moves us to stand for justice for all through His compassionate grace!"

Kelly Hall

FIRST IN THE MIND AND HEART

A True Story about the Resilience of the Human Spirit

FIRST IN THE MIND AND HEART
A True Story about the Resilience of the Human Spirit

BY
WAYLAND MATTHEW FOX

Look not mournfully into the past, it comes not back again. Wisely improve the present, it is thine. Go forth to meet the shadowy future without fear and with a manly heart.
Henry Wadsworth Longfellow

Distrust all in whom the impulse to punish is strong.
Friedrich Nietzsche

Keep me away from the wisdom which does not cry, the philosophy which does not laugh and the greatness which does not bow before children.
Khalil Gibran

LUCIDBOOKS

First in the Mind and Heart

Published by Lucid Books in Brenham, TX.
www.LucidBooks.net

First Printing 2011

ISBN-13: 9781935909088
ISBN-10: 1935909088

Special Sales: Most Lucid Books titles are available in special quantity discounts. Custom imprinting or excerpting can also be done to fit special needs. Contact Lucid Books at info@lucidbooks.net.

TABLE OF CONTENTS

ACKNOWLEDGEMENTS

Goodness can be drawn forth from hurtful circumstances. When a disaster hits, people pull together in a common effort to survive. And so it was that when my tragedy arrived, an opportunity for deepening love and faith was hidden in the crisis.

The most important way that I am able to practice recognizing the opportunity in crisis is through the loving support of the Lord, who acts through family, friends, co-workers and even strangers along the pathway of life especially in times of crisis. In difficult times, if we but try, we can find our common humanity, a link that binds us together as brothers and sisters.

I want to take this opportunity to express my gratitude to as many as possible who have been a part of this time of crisis/ opportunity in my life, without whose loving care, I would have fallen into continual despair.

Thanks to my attorney Neal Davis: You fought like a young lion in all aspects of my case, you believed in my innocence and you never gave up. I chose the right man for the job.

To my wife Sandra: You persevered against all odds, stood by my side throughout the entire ordeal, held me while I sobbed like a wounded animal in the time just following the accusation. You maintained a business without any real training, kept our home throughout my incarceration, never missed a visitation, never doubted my innocence, and kept me connected to the world, truly a spirit daughter of the Almighty and my life partner.

To my daughter Cara and family who shared money, visits and many phone calls and was a light in the darkness, and to my sons who stayed fast by my side, to my sister and family for your love, for listening to me in times of deep despair. To my own brother, my stepchildren, aunts, uncles, cousins, I can only say thank you from the bottom of my heart for your loyalty and love.

To Crosby Bean, you were constant in the early days after the accusation and hardly ever left my side, thank you. Stan Goss, thank you for spearheading the fund raising that allowed me to file the appeal which ultimately led to my release with all charges dropped. My words are empty compared to your exemplification of the literal work of Christ caring for me, your brother in my time of distress. To my friends: Kim and Diane Sawyer, Terry and Tracy Buske, Wade Quinn, David and Dorothy Williams, Don and Beverly Burton, Dwain Briggs, Bart Boyce: You came to see me again and again and again, stood in long lines waiting to visit me in jail. I can only offer my humble gratitude for your undying loyalty, your literal acting on the Masters teaching "…in jail and you visited me". Thank you Rosa Glenn Reilly for your loving consultation! You were and are a shining light in what can be treacherous psychological landscape. Thank you Dr. Roger Schultz for taking care of Sandra and I before, during and after this whole ordeal.

To all my coworkers and friends at Transworld Systems, especially Linda and John Michieli, Jim Dorn, Mike Buske, Karen Cooper, Barbara Babow, Bill Clayton, Barney Zeng and so many others who wrote to me continually, lifted my hopes, buoyed my spirit, helped me not to forget the sounds, sights, tastes of Gods creation, I owe you a tremendous debt. Thank you!

Thanks to you Bob Beare for your outrage, to you Walt Stewart for teaching me how to withstand the arrows fired at me during the trial and beyond, to Jerry Goodman for your kindness, your tears and your belief in me. And to you Stephen who saw the opportunity for humor in the whole insane spectacle of human foibles; thank you. I am grateful to Carl Schade; you watched over my property and my family and you offered a sane voice in the madness. I love you for that! Thank you to Michael Gillespie for the Urantia Book and all the letters. We go back a long way. Ann Perkins, you have taught me that life is "Rich and Full of Wonder". You are my longest held friendship on the planet. Thank you! And to all who wrote to the Grand Jury on my behalf, I will never forget!

I want to say thanks to those who befriended me and more than anyone else understood; for they lived with me in the dungeons through the horror. Thank you David Bratcher for teaching me how to survive while locked up without becoming bitter. I know the Lord has not forgotten you. Thank you to Michael Ford for your rich friendship which continues on to this day. You are my brother and friend and I will always remember you. And thank you Jose Luis Menchaca for your genuine heart, your willingness to be honest. You are a mountain of a man.

Thank you Fr. Matthew Fox for your willingness to read my working narrative and give me your quote for the book. And to you Professor David Dow, I am in your debt for reading this work and commenting. You are a force for positive evolutionary change in our world through your work in the Innocence Network.

There have been many who have contributed money, prayers, resources that I can never even completely know about. I will know you in the spirit and I am forever grateful to all who have walked with me through this test of fire.

Finally, I want to thank The Church of Jesus Christ of Latter Day Saints. Your assistance in all ways materially and spiritually has literally kept my spirit focused on the opportunity arising within this crisis; the lessons of love and service as taught by Jesus.

Wayland Matthew Fox

INTRODUCTION

This narrative is a true story, the major portion written as it unfolded over the years from March 2006 though January 2010. On December 14, 2007, I was wrongly convicted of the crime of "Indecency with a Child by Contact", a horrendous crime that I did not commit. This narrative includes the ongoing attempts to clear my name and restore my life and the subsequent victory I have won, first in the mind and heart and then on the temporal field of battle in the political maze of the judicial system. It is a story of injustice, grief and moral outrage, transcendence and the lessons of love and service through self-forgetting as taught by the Master, Jesus of Nazareth.

The preceding paragraph was written at the time of the writing of the original narrative, while I was locked in a jail cell in Harris County. I feel now that it is important to give the reader in these additional lines a glimpse into that world that most will never have to witness. It is February 22, 2011 as I now write; I have been a free man since January 14th, 2010. That is the day the prosecution finally decided to drop all charges against me, after a tooth and nail fight for my life through the complex appellate court system in this great state of Texas, a fight I won, a fight most lose.

I am forever changed by the experiences described in the pages of this narrative, never again to return to the comfort of not knowing, the naïveté of believing all that is said in the media. I am free but a part of me remains chained with those my brothers who are still fighting for a breath of fresh air, a glimpse of sunlight. I will never forget them.

This is not just my story of success, but sadly it is also the story of the left behind, the overlooked, the mentally ill, the ignorant, the dispossessed of our society who find themselves without defense in a cruel system of inhumanities, impossible odds. It is the story of the innocent and the guilty, those with power, those without power. It is a story of the human family, with all the frailties as well as the strengths found in the soul of human beings. It explores the best in the worst and the worst in the best of us.

My hope is that this writing will offer the reader a new way to contemplate the accused. Without a doubt, there are many who are rightly accused and rightly should be held accountable. But our great nation was founded on principles of "… liberty and justice for all", and "innocent until proven guilty" and it is these principles that I point at that are being trampled upon, lost in what has become a game of high stakes where lives are bargained for reputation, money, power. I only hope that we can begin to utilize common sense, fair play and to gain a higher moral ground where we are guided by justice accompanied by mercy and where our freedoms are upheld but only when tempered by responsibility.

Finally, I hope that what is most evident is the under riding theme about the possibility of love, even for ones enemies, even in horrible circumstances. This idea, taught and practiced by the Master, Jesus is eloquently stated in these great words by Paul Claudel: "There is no one of my brothers [or sisters]… that I can do without… In the heart of the meanest miser, the most squalid prostitute, the most miserable drunkard, there is an immortal soul with holy aspirations, which deprived of daylight, worships in the night. I hear them speaking when I speak and weeping when I go down on my knees. There is no one of them I can do without. Just as there are many stars in the heavens and their power of calculation is beyond my reckoning so also there are many living beings... I need them all in my praise of God. There are many living souls but there is not one of them that I'm not in communion in the sacred apex where we utter together the Our Father".

Wayland Matthew Fox

From Scripture

Deuteronomy 19:15 *(New International Version, ©2011)*

Witnesses

[15] One witness is not enough to convict anyone accused of any crime or offense they may have committed. A matter must be established by the testimony of two or three witnesses.

2 Corinthians 13:1 *(New International Version, ©2011)*

Final Warnings

[1] This will be my third visit to you. "Every matter must be established by the testimony of two or three witnesses."

Matthew 18:15-16 *(New International Version, ©2011)*

Dealing With Sin in the Church

[15] "If your brother or sister sins go and point out their fault, just between the two of you. If they listen to you, you have won them over. [16] But if they will not listen, take one or two others along, so that 'every matter may be established by the testimony of two or three witnesses.'

The Narrative as it happened.

First writings from a jail cell in mid summer 2008

BACKGROUND

My name is Wayland Matthew Fox, Jr. I am 57 years old, a Caucasian male, father of three children and the grandfather of two. I am happily married with a successful career and currently in the battle of my life to restore all that has been taken from my family and me through false allegations and a subsequent wrong conviction. This is my attempt to bring to the attention of public awareness the truth of the broken system of so called justice as I have experienced it firsthand.

God has blessed my life in overcoming great obstacles thus far, and my faith in Him remains intact. I just want my God-given life and freedom returned to me. As you read, listen in your heart for the voice of truth which always speaks for itself.

THE VISIT

On March 14, 2006 my wife answered a knock on our door around 9:00 a.m. Ms. Kennard, an investigator for Children's Protective Services, asked if I was home saying she would like to speak with me. I was at my office at the time. My wife asked to know the nature of her enquiry and was told it was regarding Jamie Tudor and his mother, Patricia Tudor, and that was all she was permitted to say. She left her card and asked my wife to have me call her as soon as possible. Patricia Tudor is my former wife, and her son, Jamie, from a previous marriage of hers, was my step-son. We had separated after four years of marriage in 2000 finalizing our divorce in 2002.

My wife Sandra called my office immediately and told me of the investigator's visit and gave me her phone number.

We both assumed something serious must have happened, and I was anxious to find out what it was. I tried to reach Ms. Kennard all day, leaving several messages and finally toward the end of the day reached her by phone. What she told me was my first knowledge of a nightmarish allegation that Jamie had made against me. He had said that I had sexually abused him on or about his 7th birthday, August 4, 1998. I soon learned what the actual allegations were and that the story changed with the different interviews he went through. He claimed that on several occasions, while at home alone with me, I came into his room (later, in another interview, said I took him to my room), had him undress, (one story had just his shirt off and another his pants pulled down), caused him to lie face down on the bed and that I straddled him and rubbed my penis on his bare back. Other variations of his claims were that I touched his penis, or rubbed my penis on his buttocks. He was 14 years old at the time of this allegation, close to 7 years after these events were supposed to have happened.

After the initial shock of just finding out I was accused of a sex crime, and before I knew what the actual allegations were, I came to my senses and asked what she wanted, telling her unequivocally that whatever it was didn't happen. Ms. Kennard said she would like for me to come in to her office for an interview and wondered what would be a good time for me. Without any thought, I told her I would come right away as I wanted to get to the bottom of this. She agreed to see me that afternoon, March 14th, 2006. I drove home and picked up my wife and we started out toward the location across town.

On the way, I decided to call the civil attorney who was handling an auto accident claim for my wife. When I reached him, he told me forcefully not to go to the meeting without an attorney. I became frightened as some of the reality and the implications of this accusation began to sink in. I then called the investigator back and told her I would need to consult with an attorney before any interview could take place. She said that would be fine and to give her a call at such time when I was ready. Not being as of yet charged with a crime, it was my right to refuse the interview. Though I took the advice of the civil attorney, I was anxious for this interview to take place so as to clear up any wrong statements being made about me as soon as possible.

SEEKING ADVICE/HELP

This began the process of seeking counsel. After reaching out to several close friends over the next couple days, I was put in contact with Peter Ferris, a member of The Mankind Project. I also belong to this worldwide organization that has a mission of making the world a better place. Peter is a criminal attorney here in Houston, and I'd met him previously at one of the events sponsored by The Mankind Project. After telling him my story as I knew it so far, he offered to make some calls to see what he could find out. This was the beginning of my knowledge of what the specific allegations were, "how" they came about, and the seriousness of the situation I faced. I have yet to discover or be informed "why" the allegations were made. As to "why", I can only speculate. Let me explain further and perhaps you too will speculate.

THE RELATIONSHIPS

I met Patricia (Jamie's mother) in November or December of 1993. We had both been invited to a meeting to help plan a going away party for a mutual friend who was moving back to his home in Israel. Initially, there was a physical attraction

23

between us that was obvious. I was 41 years old then and she was 36 so we both had enough maturity to recognize the chemistry.

Patricia was still married but estranged; she and her husband were still living in the same home in separate bedrooms, or so I was told by Patricia. She said they were staying together out of mutual financial concerns. Jamie, their son, was two years old at the time. The physical attraction between Patricia and I was very strong and I admit that I did go against my own values when we decided to see each other.

It did not take long before our relationship became sexual; and if my memory serves me right, I moved Patricia and Jamie in with my two sons and me within the first couple months. My sons Jeffrey and Robert were 10 and 8 years old at the time. When I met Patricia, I had already gained full custody of my sons following a divorce from their mother in 1986 so I had already been raising them by myself seven years when I took on the role of stepfather to Jamie. Being active with my sons in scouting and every form of sport, it was natural for me to bring Jamie up in that same fashion. I was on the go with him in baseball, basketball, soccer and scouts from the time he was old enough to participate and throughout his elementary school years.

Unfortunately, and it has taken me too long to learn this; a relationship which is only based on the natural chemistry between a man and woman usually results in failure when no real friendship has been developed prior to cohabitating. At least, that has been my experience. The first year with Patricia was the fun of falling in love, but when the real issues of life appeared, we began to have problems. At first our so called "love" for each other was enough to endure the intense power struggles, but eventually, we became caught up in an unending, impossible emotional battle that lasted until the year 2000 when we separated. We had even married in 1997. I remember thinking the commitment alone would help us to work things out!

Please understand, there were happy times too but as the years went by, the complications resulting from our efforts to blend our families far outweighed our good times. Without going into detail about these complications and ***without blame of any kind***, we simply were not equipped to manage the complexity of mother/child, father/child, mother/stepchild, father/stepchild, mother/father/stepchild/child, brother/ brother, brother/stepbrother, etc., etc. You get my point. Complicating all of this and, again, not in a spirit of blame, Patricia and I had baggage from previous marriages which still burdened us both.

Notwithstanding all the challenges, we both worked hard to resolve our difficulties, even seeking out therapy and being involved in support groups to address the issues we faced. Jamie hugged me and called me Daddy, ran and clung to me when scared, and cried and laughed with me. I was his Dad and his coach and tried to be good at both.

Patricia and I had differences of opinion about parenting at times, as many couples do. But in the more serious difficulties, there was a tendency for Patricia and Jamie to retreat to one corner and my sons and I to another and it became "us against them". We were just never able to get past the tribulations and both Patricia and I had careers which brought additional power struggles in the areas of finances, responsibilities, home care, etc., etc. To say that the children of this blended family were able to withstand the ups and downs of those years without any effect on the building of their characters would be an absolute case of serious denial. All I can say, in terms of any redemption of those years of trouble, is that Patricia and I both tried to take responsibility for our individual contributions to the dysfunction of our relationship. We would resolve our fights; we just could not stop starting the fights!

ALCOHOL AND DRUG FREE - SOBRIETY AND DEFENSE

I want to tell you about my life as a recovered alcoholic and what I have found to be absolutely imperative for me to remain clean and sober, as well as free of any sort of immorality as is suggested by the charges against me. I won't go into the long log of events prior to my getting sobered up on April 1, 1985. Suffice it to say, in the last years before that date; I was bankrupt physically, mentally, emotionally, and spiritually. I reached the last house on the block, Alcoholics Anonymous. AA lays out a spiritual program of recovery and by embracing the principles of the AA program I lead an alcohol and drug free life and have done so for 23 plus years.

The first and most important principle I <u>must</u> live by is honesty, and I must live by it to as great and deep a degree as is humanly possible. For me to allow any form of dishonesty is a set-up for relapse, as millions in AA will testify. The next principle is an ongoing daily self-examination to search out and be rid of the flaws in my character that were my downfall for years prior to getting sober. The next principle is faith in and dependence upon God for all my needs and an ongoing attempt to maintain a conscious contact with Him so as to stay free from the bondage of self. The last principle is that of being of service to my fellow man. As one who has recovered, I have much to offer to the man who still suffers.

I have tried my best to live according to these principles, and I am now undergoing a profound testing of this hard won faith. I say all of this to make it absolutely clear to my readers that it would not be possible for me to remain sober or sane had I committed such a horrendous and violent act as sexual abuse of a child. For the sober addict/alcoholic there are three MUSTS – Trust God, Clean House and Help Others - and the sobriety that I have is the gift of God and is contingent on the daily maintenance of my spiritual condition through adherence to these principles. For me it is a life or death question and I chose to live long ago.

I hope you will understand that while the statements above may sound self-serving, it is in fair defense against the outrageous accusations against me. I have not been able to maintain perfect adherence to the principles but I do claim progress in the spiritual life and the effort to correct mistakes when I make them. This amend-making process is another "must" if I would remain sober. The sober alcoholic cannot live long with guilt, dishonesty, resentment or fear and stay sober.

This brings me to an explanation of "how" the accusation occurred and the speculation of "why" it occurred. These details of the accusation I learned from the initial attorney who advised me, the subsequent CPS interview, the indictment, and finally from my present attorney who represented me in the trial and is continuing to do so in the appeal.

THE FACTS OF HOW / SPECULATION OF WHY

"*How*" the accusation came about may cause the reader, as it did me, to speculate as to "why" the accuser made such a terrible accusation. To begin, I had not seen Jamie or his mother since 2002, four years before the allegation except at the trial that occurred in December 2007. As I mentioned, Patricia and I were separated in 2000 and the divorce became final in 2002. In the year just after separation, I had a number of visits with Jamie. I had been his Dad from the age of two until the age of nine, seven years, and I wanted to continue to maintain contact with him if he also wanted the same.

Sometime in that year, Jamie and his mother relocated to a city over ninety miles away from Houston. I was not told where and so had lost complete contact with Jamie. I consequently inquired among friends, was able to locate them and finally spoke to Patricia making her aware that I wished to continue to have contact with Jamie. I told her I did not want him to feel abandoned by me. Prior to this, Jamie and I had written letters to each other and his love for me as his stepfather was obvious in the letters. She agreed and said Jamie could come as long as he wanted to visit me and so he came on a Saturday for his first and only visit after the move in the summer of 2002.

We had a great time together that day as Jamie played in the yard with the dogs he'd known before at our home and with familiar neighborhood kids that were close to his age. They came over and played pool together in the house for a while and Jamie even asked the boys' mother if they could spend the night at "his dad's" (my) house. All in all it was a very pleasant visit and when his mother arrived to take him home, we hugged each other and talked of our next visit as we said our goodbyes.

Earlier that year, I had begun dating Sandra (now my wife) and prior to the time of Jamie's visit, Sandra had come to live with me. The evening after Jamie had returned home from our visit, I got a call from his mother. Having learned from Jamie about Sandra being in my home, Patricia was furious and called to tell me Jamie would never come to visit me again. I tried to reason with her, thinking of Jamie and how he would feel and what he wanted, but her mind was made up. I never saw him again, and no longer being his relative in any legal sense, I had no choice but to let him go. This was very difficult for me because I had raised him for 7 years as my son. Hence, my speculation is that he felt and still feels abandoned by me, his father figure from age two to nine. This story could be his way of enacting revenge in the perception that I had caused him and his mother pain. She testified in the trial that the divorce and the subsequent time had been painfully difficult.

In February 2006 when Jamie was 14, and just prior to my being contacted by CPS, there was a motivational speaker who gave a series of talks to the student body of the school where Jamie attended. As I understand through the efforts of my attorney, and in studying the transcripts of the actual trial, the speaker's talks included content about the emerging sexuality of children and upholding the virtue of remaining a virgin until married. He even asked kids to stand up if they were still virgin and he would hand out gifts like t-shirts, socks, books and even tennis shoes – things that would appeal to most 14-year-old kids. With this done, he asked if there was anyone who had ever had anything happen to them which they might be afraid to discuss such as inappropriate sexual contact. If so, they should come forward after the talk and speak with a counselor. Let me say that these were the events as they were told to me through the investigation done by my attorney, and not being there, I cannot validate the exact sequence of these events. Jamie did however at some point approach the staff of the speaker with his story of alleged sexual abuse by me.

A bit of history on Jamie that may clarify the type of child he was: His real father who continued relatively regular contact with Jamie throughout my relationship with Patricia spent many years as an actor at the Texas Renaissance Festival. Each year from a very young age when the festival would come through town, Jamie would be taken to the festival by his mother and his father, and he grew up learning the skills of being an actor. During elementary and middle school, Jamie would continue to learn the skills of acting by performing in plays and he won many awards doing so. There were many times throughout his childhood when he would call us, the family, together to watch him perform scenes that he would fabricate from his own wondrous and vivid imagination. He was a very precocious child. He preferred to be with adults a lot of times, and when with others his own age, insisted on having things done his own way. At the same time, he could be quite happy and generous and even compromising when asked to try another way besides just his own.

After coming forward with the initial allegation, the information he had given to the staff of the speaker was relayed to a school counselor who instructed Jamie that he needed to tell his mother. It later came out in the trial that at some point Jamie told his mother that he was afraid that he was gay and expressed that he did not want to be. This is another cause for speculation as to "why" he would make up such a story. Also, another cause for speculation introduced in trial was that Jamie was given gifts: he received a new pair of tennis shoes; a bag of socks; and some books after coming forward with his story. And there were many different versions of this story that he would tell at various times in interviews with officers and counselors. I will not go into the details again about these varying stories or the allegations, except to say the charge was Indecency with a Child. My first indictment said Indecency by Exposure, but was later changed to read Indecency by Contact. Other than this 14-year-old boy's word of mouth, there is not one person, professional or other to verify his story.

The idea that an adult man's life can be completely destroyed simply on the words of another without eyewitness or evidence to prove beyond the shadow of a doubt, is anti-American in my mind. The prevailing attitude both in Child Protective Services and in the general public is that children do not lie about these occurrences. Do not forget that on a recent television documentary, a man spent 20 years in a California prison on the words of a child and the child when grown re-canted saying that he had lied and that the abuse had never happened. The man was released, but he will never be able to have the 20 years of his freedom, his life, that were lost on the false words of a child. Please, do the research yourself - false allegations, false memory syndrome, vengeful ex-spouses who manipulate children into telling lies, etc., etc. There are more and more examples of these phenomena emerging all the time.

THE INTERVIEW

So I made a decision against the advice of the civil attorney I had talked with to go in to the CPS interview knowing that this allegation was a fabrication. Because I am innocent, I was anxious to go in and surely after speaking with me, they would absolutely know the allegation was false. My acquaintance from the Mankind Project, the criminal attorney I mentioned, was unsure if it was a good idea and he quite frankly did not want to get too much more involved unless I hired him. The reality was that I did not have the kind of money needed to hire him. So, I decided I would go for the interview believing naively that truth would prevail in the short run. I regret that decision to this day. If any of you ever find yourself in a similar position, never go to an interview with law enforcement if you are suspected of a crime without a criminal defense attorney, and I mean NEVER! The interview was videotaped without my knowledge. It was conducted by a police officer and the investigator who originally contacted me. A lot of information about my life had been given to the police by my former wife who knew my history of alcoholism and recovery and many other private, intimate husband/wife details that were later used illegally in my trial. Thus my grounds for appeal are good, but never certain in our broken legal system. So, I told the truth. I told way too much truth about my life, as I had no shame since I had spent the last 20 plus years trying to correct the problems stemming from my life prior to recovery from alcoholism. After the interview, the officer asked if I would take a polygraph. I agreed I would and the officer said to give her a call in a day or two to set it up and I did this as well.

THE INDICTMENT, THE BOND, THE BROKEN SYSTEM

A couple weeks had passed since the interview, maybe a month, and we found out that the officer who interviewed me would be seeking an indictment and therefore a warrant was issued for my arrest. I immediately contacted a bonding company and they located the warrant that had been issued. They told me my bond had been set at $30,000.00. I was told to meet the bonding agent at the location downtown where bonds are posted. She said I should lay low somewhere until she could make it there. I was terrified. I met the bonding agent there at 4:00 p.m. and I was walked through a process, fingerprinted, photographed and released on bond. I had to pay $3000.00 to the bonding company. Restrictions were placed on my freedom which I have since learned is a violation of my "Sixth amendment to the Constitution" right. It was a violation because these restrictions had been placed on me as a result of an adversarial hearing that was held without me or an attorney for my defense present. Please see the U.S. Supreme Court Ruling in Rothgery vs. Gillespie County, TX. Case Number 07-440, argued on March 17, 2008, decided June 23, 2008. Let me say here that my belief that my rights have been violated is my opinion based on my own interpretation of the Supreme Court Ruling. All law is subject to interpretation, hence the existence of the appellate court system and the U.S. Supreme Court. Read it for yourself. I was never notified of my right to a "preliminary hearing", which in Texas is called and "examining trial". And this right was supposed to be made known to me at an "article 15.17" hearing. See Texas Criminal Proc. Code Ann, Art. 15.17 (a).

I was never notified of or present at any such hearing, another violation since all of my constitutional protections as a defendant were attached as soon as I was fingerprinted, photographed and posted bond.

SEEKING LEGAL COUNSEL

After much discussion with friends and family, I started the process of finding an attorney to represent me should I be indicted. I met with five different attorneys. After telling each of them my story, the whole story as I knew it, I asked two questions of each. The questions were: "Why are you an attorney?" and "Does it matter to you if your client is innocent?" I had good reason for asking these questions. The answers I got to the first question were very telling. Most of the men answered that they loved the idea of the drama of the courtroom. They were taken aback by the question, saying they had never been asked such. I actually was trying to find out what, if any, noble purpose other than making a good living was their motivation for being an attorney. One of them told me he loved being in front of a trial jury. I responded by saying "Obviously you have a vested interest (his ego) in this case getting to trial". The man was stunned. I did not hire him, though he was considered one of the better attorneys. He actually called me the next day saying he had not been able to stop thinking about my question. He wanted to offer his services at a reduced rate. I declined.

The second question was important to me because I wanted an attorney who would be more interested in the truth, which is what our system of justice is supposed to be seeking. All but one of the five said it did not matter to them if their client was innocent. One even told me "An innocent man is my worst nightmare". His reasoning for this was that if he lost, he would have to live with this knowledge. He was not a good candidate in my mind. One should obviously know the terrain he is entering into before making a career decision. I finally decided on a young liberal attorney who had been noted in the newspapers as being a go-getter. His responses to my two questions satisfied me. He said he became an attorney because he had the kind of mind for it and he liked the idea of helping people in trouble. He also said it was important to him to know whether his client was innocent or not. I trusted him from the beginning. It is important that the client trusts his attorney and vice versa for a good case to be made in one's defense. Even with the best defense attorney, in cases such as these, where only someone's word with no other evidence can send a person to prison for life, the innocent man or woman can and many times do lose. I must assume based on my experience that there are many now in our jails and prisons that are innocent. The adversarial system does not care about the truth; the game is to win at all costs.

PSYCHOLOGICAL EVALUATIONS & CHARACTER REFERENCES

I contracted with Mr. Neal Davis in order for him to represent me throughout the trial if necessary. The contractual fee was $50,000.00 to be pre-paid, plus expenses for investigation, a three day psychological evaluation and a polygraph test. I passed both the evaluation and the polygraph.

This money which took our entire savings and all of the equity in our home would not cover a re-trial or any appellate process in the event of a mistrial or conviction. The fee covered only the services rendered through the end of the initial trial.

After contracting with Neal, my wife and I met with him to discuss my case. This along with subsequent meetings led to a full disclosure of my entire life, as much as I could remember. In addition, my attorney arranged to have an independent psychological evaluation by a local psychologist renowned in the area of my type of charge. This evaluation included a battery of tests occurring over a three-day period and a one on one interview with him where I again disclosed all major, as well as, many of the minor events of my life. The testing and interview resulted in the doctor's professional written opinion that I absolutely did not fit any (so called) profile of a sex offender and that the prosecution in my case should look elsewhere for their "sex offender". This information was never presented in court. Neither was the information that I had passed the polygraph test. The doctor was never even called to testify. I do believe, however, that my attorney had good reason, some of it being legal restriction and some being part of his defense strategy. The procedure and drama of the courtroom is complex and not easy to fathom from a lay perspective. I trusted my attorney then and I still do, as I have contracted with him again for my appeals process.

Since we knew the case would be going to the grand jury for consideration, I embarked on an effort to gather character reference letters from close friends, family members, people who had known me for many, many years, professionals including psychotherapists in the field of sex abuse whom I personally knew, lawyers whom I knew, a minister from my church, an appellate judge working in Louisiana Family Services, and a best-selling author who wrote on the field of child abuse, addiction and recovery and family systems dynamics. I had worked for this author for eight years. Working with him acquainted me with many people in psychotherapeutic circles and was a direct result of and is a continuing influence in my recovery from alcoholism and drug addiction. My entire life since 1985 has been an effort to raise consciousness about issues such as child abuse and it is indeed ironic that I now find myself falsely accused and wrongfully convicted of such a horrendous crime. I received thirty plus letters from people I referenced above attesting to my character and asking the Grand Jury to "no bill" this case. The two psychotherapists were present at the Grand Jury hearing to be available for questioning in my defense. The Grand Jury decided against hearing them. I was not present, at my attorney's advice, but was later told that little attention was paid to the letters of reference and that the Grand Jury had returned with a true-bill. I have since learned that 99% of all alleged sex abuse cases are true-billed and sent to the courts to sort the "truth" out. This may be somewhat understandable from a human nature perspective as they obviously don't want to make a mistake and release a real child predator, so they just rubber stamp these types of cases to let the courts decide. In other words, they pass the buck.

My attorney's efforts to talk to Jaimie's mother failed. She just would not take his call. I still believe to this day that she knows in her heart that this allegation is false and I further believe that both Patricia and Jaimie are experiencing a torment of soul as a result of Jamie's making a false accusation, and that eventually they will have to come to terms with truth as all people must do within their own hearts and souls. I want more than anything that if it be God's will, once I am released, I will have an opportunity to restore the relationship that I once had and failed to continue to fight for with my ex step-son.

THE POLYGRAPH

It is no wonder that polygraph tests are not allowed in the courts as part of a trial process as they can be extremely unreliable. Go on the Internet yourself and see the groups that are fighting against their use, even as an investigative tool or as a tool used for people on probation. Why they are even allowed at all is a travesty of justice. I have met men who because of a polygraph taken while on parole or probation have found themselves back in jail, most without the means to afford counsel. My own experience was terrifying but ultimately gave me great hope. However, the hope was short lived when the prosecutor ignored the result. Do you suppose it would have been ignored had it showed that I was lying?

The person we chose to do the polygraph was a thirty year veteran professional and my attorney and my wife were both present. My attorney and the polygraphist met to come up with the formulated questions, which are so incredibly important. For instance, the question "Did you ever show your penis to your step-son?" is a confusing question. The answer is of course "yes" as I have urinated beside him both in the woods on camping trips and even side by side in the toilet as fathers and sons will sometimes do. A great fear arises with this question because it is assumed they want a "no" answer. Consider the question phrased this way, "Did you ever show your penis to your step-son (name) for the purpose of sexual gratification?" A good attorney will be in on the formulation of such questions to protect his client. There are polygraphists who will ask questions the first way that I mentioned which can cause great consternation particularly for the innocent.

Upon completion of the test and after showing the results to the attorney, the polygraphist came out where I was waiting and said "No wonder you were so nervous, you are innocent." I learned from him, a thirty-year veteran in his field, that innocent people have a much harder time with testing than ones who are guilty. The nervousness of such a person who is brand new to this process can cause problems with the machinery. I was absolutely troubled by having to be asked such questions to begin with, but enormously relieved in the subsequent discussion with the polygraphist.

THE DEPRESSION, THE HORROR, THE GOODNESS

I'm going to backtrack here for a moment. The time after the CPS interview, and especially after learning they would be seeking an indictment, I reached what I felt was the most difficult and lowest time of my entire life. However, I have since known even lower and more difficult times considering where I have been for the last year and now waiting for my appeal to begin. While on bond and waiting for a trial date, I became so extremely depressed that my wife took me to a doctor who almost hospitalized me. The doctor prescribed an anti-depressant and I began seeing a therapist and with the aid of both, I was able to continue on. I have great compassion now for those who suffer from clinical depression. It is like being imprisoned in one's own mind with no way out, a truly horrible way to be. A family doctor, also a friend, had written a letter of reference attesting to my character and knowing my financial situation saw me and helped me at no cost. I had no insurance either, as I had my own commission only sales business. He continues even to this day providing medical services to my wife at no charge. There are obviously still good people in this world. There are many high points in my overall experience of this crisis in which the best in people has emerged. They came together. They built community around a just cause and bonds were forged or deepened that continues to enhance lives today in ways both temporal and eternal.

FIRST COURT APPEARANCE

Backtracking now to the initial time of my arrest, I had made bond and my first court appearance was scheduled. I don't recall the exact date of this first appearance and at that time I had as of yet not hired an attorney. I went to court on that day with the foreknowledge that the judge would grant me time to find and hire an attorney. My dignity was assaulted when the judge allowed an open court vocal reading of the explicit details of the charges that had been brought against me, and this was allowed without me having an attorney present. Many other people were present in the court for various other cases. One man even approached me in the hall outside the courtroom afterward and started yelling in my face "child molester" as well as other threatening, degrading remarks which I will not recite here.

The judge, after hearing my "not guilty" plea asked if I needed an attorney or if I would be hiring one. I said I would hire one and when asked how much time I would need, I asked for 90 days. She retorted in a very angry tone that she would not allow such a ridiculous amount of time and proceeded to grant me 30 days. The idea that a man or woman is presumed innocent until proven guilty (a constitutional guarantee) is no longer applicable in my beloved America. In my experience, judges (particularly in Texas) are in league with prosecutors to win convictions, not to seek the truth. Go to a Texas courtroom trial and make your own observation. The people need to "wake up" from their sleeping. The truth as I now see it is that many Americans with our color televisions and air conditioning and Jack Daniels whiskey have been lulled to sleep in our comforts while our very beloved "Bill of Rights" as guaranteed by our constitution is under attack and since most are asleep to this reality, this goes largely unnoticed. If I sound preachy, you must understand that my life is at stake and not only my life but also the lives of my children, grandchildren and on into the future. I have a spiritual and moral obligation to speak out against the obvious decline of our moral fiber. Ignorance is no excuse in our present day age of information. Please, for the sake of our world now and in the future…seek and you shall find! Again, when I speak of our moral fiber, I mean our dedication to truth above all…at all costs! Judges and prosecutors care about convictions and re-election. The people are mostly asleep!

COURTROOM POLITICS/NEW JUDGE ASSIGNED

As a condition of my bond, the judge placed many restrictions on me. Why was I restricted if I was supposed innocent until proven guilty? She required me to come weekly for a urinalysis, which I paid for out of my own pocket for about eight months or so. I passed all of them. She also required that I not have any contact with anyone under the age of 17 years. I was not allowed to see my grandchildren, go near schools, daycares, parks or anywhere children might gather. I am self-employed and the majority of my business is handled through Internet web services where my customers place orders online. The judge took away my right to have Internet in my home. Fortunately, I also have an office away from home and she begrudgingly allowed me access at my office. The loss of Internet at home affected my wife and her son who is 25 and lives with us. He was starting a computer repair business and needed access to work online. I was also restricted from going more than 100 miles from home without court permission. These restrictions continued for close to a full year.

At some strategic point and after having many court appearances, only to be rescheduled again and again because the prosecution was not prepared, my attorney revealed to the judge who the proprietor of my chosen law firm was. It turns out that the judge was under investigation for prosecutorial misconduct and that the proprietor of the law firm I chose (a high profile attorney in Houston) was her chief accuser. When she learned of this news, she immediately excused herself from my case refusing to hear it. My case was then assigned to another courtroom, another prosecutor (the third or fourth by this time) and a different judge.

When the judge reviewed my file and found me in total compliance with the court for approximately an entire year, all of my restrictions were removed. It was a great day of joy when I was reunited with my grandchildren. I was allowed Internet access in my home again and I could go and travel wherever I wanted. Nevertheless, a great sensitivity to children encompassed my entire being bordering on fear. I was almost afraid to hug my grandchildren when they ran to jump into my arms. This sensitivity has never left me and probably never will. Children are naturally intuitive and can sense when something has changed. What a tragedy when a man feels compelled to modify the natural expression of his love for his grandchildren. I hope you are getting this. My life has been forever altered by the lie of another person. My grandchildren's lives have also been forever altered. Do you see? Are you awake?

THE TRIAL

The whole ordeal had begun with that knock on my door on March 14, 2006. The following nineteen months on bond was a horrendous rollercoaster ride of heartache, depression, incredible family stress with the occasional success which kept hope alive. This hope was embodied in the unity of friends, family and business colleagues who stood by me, poured out their hearts to me, held me up when I could not stand. This love in action continues even to this very day.

The trial date was finally set for December 10, 2007. We had selected a number of witnesses, some who were in my life at the time of the alleged abuse and others who had met me later that were called strictly as character witnesses. The prosecution brought the child, the mother and the authorities from CPS and law enforcement who had interviewed them. There was not one piece of physical evidence, not one person to say that they had ever seen or heard of any inappropriate behavior in my relationship with Jaimie. In fact, all testimony revealed that I was always appropriate around children. Even his mother admitted, when questioned, that I had been a good father to her son. This child is now 16 years old and I have no idea whatsoever how he maintains this horrible lie within his own heart and soul. I had witnesses and supporters that filled more than two rows in the courtroom. Included were my own sons and daughter who came to support me for the entire trial.

December 10, 2007 is a day burned into my awareness that will not soon be forgotten. The memory is somewhat dreamlike now or maybe I should say nightmarish. The judge who normally presided over the courtroom happened to be on, I'm assuming, his holiday vacation, so a visiting judge was sent in to hear the case. This was a complete surprise but one about which we had no say. This judge who had absolutely no idea of who I was, what I had endured up until this point in time or what this case was about was sent in to preside and help determine my future fate. He is from Austin and from what I've been told he has been barred from sitting on the bench there. His rulings have been overturned on many occasions by the appellate courts. He is a retired ex-marine, and a cigar smoking conservative judge that looked to be in his mid to late seventies. Being retired, he only sits in as a visiting judge and I believe that is primarily in Houston.

We immediately saw the new judge's pro-prosecution stance as objection after objection by my attorney was overruled without any thought. There were events in my life from forty years in the past, when I was still in my teenage years, as well as more recent intimate details of my sex life with the mother of the complainant who had been my wife at that time. These details that were supposedly "not to be allowed as evidence" were allowed by the judge anyway. At one point, my attorney threw up his hands and asked for a running objection on the entire line of questioning being asked at the time. In the final argument, the prosecution argued to the jury that they "could" consider my past to determine if I was guilty. In Texas Rules of Evidence 401 and 404 this practice is illegal. "A person is not to be tried on the basis of who he was or even is, but only on facts surrounding the allegations". The prosecutor continued saying "Those kinds of things may absolutely weigh in who Matthew Fox is today…"

I suppose it is important for me to talk to you of these things that the court had initially agreed to have withheld from trial as evidence through a "Motion in Limine" filed by my attorney. This is a term meaning that the information would not be allowed in trial. This agreement had been made between my attorney, the judge and the prosecutor in a pretrial hearing when all the motions on both sides were reviewed in the presence of the judge who was to preside over the case. I have since learned that any information is admissible in a court of law unless someone objects. A pretrial hearing is usually held to pre-determine just what objections might arise from supposed evidence gathered by either side. It is in this manner that motions are filed to withhold certain "so called" evidence from being used in the court.

One of the events that my ex-wife had conveyed to the CPS investigator and then to the Prosecutor that had occurred in my life and that was supposedly not to be allowed in the trial happened when I was seventeen. I was coaxed into having a homosexual experience with a man twice my age. He had been recommended to me to interview for a summer job just after high school putting together displays in a department store. The man was a gifted artist and I had been referred to him by my art teacher in high school. This man showered me with gifts, praise, much needed attention, and I eventually gave into his advances for sex in return for the job as well as all the gifts which included fancy clothes, trips to other cities, exciting conversations with older people etc, etc. This was a very damaging experience that caused great confusion in my developing mind and spirit. It took a lot of therapy later in my life to work through the anger and hurt that I carried as a result of that experience. But that is the point. I worked through it and resolved it. The argument from the prosecutor was that I had this predilection to homosexuality. On the contrary, it was a disgusting experience and left no doubt as to my nature as a heterosexual male. The idea that an experience from 40 years prior could be used as supposed evidence of having committed a crime is indeed preposterous but would certainly have potential to prejudice a jury in weighing character when dramatized by the antics of a prosecutor looking only for a win and not for the truth.

There was additional information allowed in the trial which was supposed to have been held in limine (not allowable in trial) due to its inflammatory nature and its capacity to prejudice the jury and lead them away from the facts of the case. This information was allowed after multiple objections from my attorney and after a decision by the judge who said that one of my attorneys questions to my ex wife opened the door to allowing the information in. The Appellate Court later disagreed with the judge.

The information was this: There had been times in my past when I had experimented with cross-dressing. One time in my marriage to Patricia, I had playfully slipped on one of her negligees and approached her in the bedroom. It was all in fun and playfulness. She did not seem to have a negative reaction to it and not much ever came of it. There has never been any need to go out in public dressed as a woman, or do anything outside of the privacy of my own home and certainly not any connection to any desire to hurt or abuse children or anyone else for that matter. But when this information was allowed to be presented to the jury, and in a way that made me out to be some kind of freak through an over dramatization by the prosecution, it obviously carried a great potential to paint my character in an abnormal light.

The appellate court later ruled that the information was not in any way connected with the allegation and therefore was highly inflammatory and had the capacity to sway a jury toward making a connection between cross-dressing and abusing children sexually. We do not know what went on in the deadlocked hours in the jury chamber with regards to this information but the outcome of the case can only lead one to speculate about how the information may have prejudiced the jury against me. In the evaluation done by a professional psychologist, he could find no connection between this behavior and sex abuse and in short order in his written statement to the court stated that the prosecution needed to look elsewhere for their child predator.

The jury began deliberating at 2:00 p.m. December 13, 2007. At 4:51 p.m., the jury sent a note out to the judge that stated "We are currently split on a decision and see we will have significant difficulties at this time reaching a unanimous verdict. Please offer your comments or direction." The trial court judge instructed jurors to continue deliberating.

At 6:32 p.m. the jury asked for a read back of testimony. On a form the trial court provided, the jury was asked to specify which portion of testimony was in dispute. The jury requested on the form the prosecutions direct examination of the complainant regarding his "description of the abuse, what he saw and where he went to". My attorney Neal provided the trial court with the case Jones vs State, 706 S.W. 2d 664 (Texas Criminal Appeals, 1986) and asked that the complainant's relevant cross-examination also be read back to the jury. This request was denied because the trial court did not "want to comment on the weight". The appellate courts had already reversed a decision in the Jones vs State case where the same issue occurred. In my case as in the Jones', the jury was deprived of having the relevant cross-examination which made my entire trial unfair by law. The court reporter read to the jury the complainant's "relevant" direct examination only.

Close to 9:00 p.m., after seven hours of deliberation, the jury sent a note stating it was "hopelessly deadlocked". The trial court gave an "Allen Charge" which is the legal term for a pep talk by the judge to the jury emphasizing that they are under an obligation to reach a unanimous decision. This is not true due to the fact that there have been mistrials declared because of deadlocks. Shortly thereafter, the jury was released with instructions to return the next morning at 9:00 a.m. to continue deliberating.

The next morning, December 14, 2007, the jury, after going through the entire process of jury selections, going back and forth to the courthouse for several days and many long hours of trial, having previously struggled through seven hours of deliberations (Not to mention that there were only eleven days left until Christmas and it was now Friday.), returned a guilty verdict after just one hour. The trial had degenerated into a spectacle of the prosecution's effort to humiliate me, assassinating my character based on forty years prior, and appealing to the jurors' emotion and prejudice rather than their reason and common sense. The difficulty the jury had in reaching a verdict indicated that the jury struggled with whether I was guilty. Had this irrelevant testimony been excluded as it should have been according to the law, the jury may well have never reached a verdict or may even have acquitted me.

They then went into the punishment phase of the trial which the jury also deliberated on. After a short period of time, the jury returned with a ten year sentence; the minimum was two years, the maximum was 20. They went down the middle. I was absolutely devastated and dumbfounded as I was taken out of the courtroom and moved into the dehumanizing process of being incarcerated in the Harris County Jail where I sit now to write my story.

September 25, 2008

THE DARK AGES/SPIRIT

After a couple days of sitting in holding tanks, I was taken through a series of tunnels into other buildings. The tunnels I later discovered went under the streets of downtown Houston. To this day, I don't know exactly where

I am. It is very disconcerting to have no sense of direction, to be lost as it were in a maze. I was given an orange jumpsuit, a pair of shower sandals, a towel, two sets of underwear, a bag with a bar of soap, a very tiny toothbrush and a small tube of some kind of toothpaste. I went through a process of being put into more holding cells with 20-40 other inmates waiting for tank assignment. I witnessed horrible violence in one of these holding cells. There was absolutely no supervision during these times. I had been taking an anti-depressant and an anxiety medication for close to a year prior to being jailed. To no avail, I told the authorities of my need for these medications during those hours of processing (more on this later). Sometime after midnight, I was given a thin green mattress, a sheet and bedspread and taken to the fifth floor. Once there I was escorted through a couple of electronic steel doors and found myself in tank 5F-1 which is where I am now.

I have now been incarcerated for nine and a half months without sunshine, eating a diet mostly of carbohydrates with very little fruit or vegetables. I have limited access to exercise that includes only three hours per week of volleyball and which is too aggressive for someone my age. This particular tank has six individual cells holding eight bunks each. Each cell opens to a dayroom when their barred gates are opened electronically by the guards. Though there are only 48 bunks, the tank always has 50 to 60 men. The guards bring in portable cots for the extra men, making it a violation of federal standards for county facilities. The individual cells which hold 8 men each are approximately 12x24 feet in size. Each cell has eight double deck bunks made of steel that are bolted to the concrete floor and ceiling and brick walls. There is a single open toilet and sink. We are locked in these cells from 10 p.m. to 7 a.m. Sunday through Thursday and on Friday and Saturday from 12 a.m. to 7 a.m.

We are served a breakfast around 4 a.m. consisting of a highly sugared cereal, a pint of milk, a piece of fruit and/or a boiled egg. Sometimes chocolate covered packaged donuts are served and much trading occurs when they are. Occasionally we get raisin bran, the only one I'll eat because it actually has some nutritional value. Most of the men will then go back to sleep until 7 a.m. when we are assaulted by loudspeakers and bright lights to get us up for the daily count. The electronic gated cell doors are then opened to the day room and we can go out of our cells or stay in, whatever we choose. Our beds have to be made and we are not allowed to get into the covers again until 10 p.m. or midnight, depending on the day.

We are also given a plastic bag to hold our personal belongings such as we have for personal hygiene, commissary, books, paper and pens which are made of rubber. We are also allowed an electric plastic container for heating water to make coffee, instant cocoa or Ramen Noodle soup, which are all purchased through commissary if we are lucky enough to have money to do so.

Inmates can be quite creative saving leftovers and creating what are called "spreads" which include as the base, Ramen soup noodles. One of the "spreads" we make is chicken tortilla soup, a mixture of leftover canned corn, peas or green beans with a few tortilla chips and small amount of cheese added at the very last can make quite a tasty meal. There have been quite a number of different recipes thought up for those who are able to have money to purchase commissary. Spaghetti happens to be one of my favorites as we get meatballs a couple times a month and can put together a make shift spaghetti meal with commissary items. We also try to save up as much as we can and we will make a large fruit salad to be shared among those in our cell, usually eight or nine men.

The sharing that goes on here is quite impressive. There is also a lot of trading that goes on daily. Food is the main medium of exchange and is used just like it is money. There are disputes over these transactions, just as there are monetary disputes in the free world, usually involving debit/credit transactions. Drugs are commonly traded, everything from strong sleeping medications to narcotics. I'll elaborate more on this subject later.

As mentioned previously, the cells are all open to a day room that is approximately 15ft. x 60ft. in size. On the far wall opposite the cells, there is a windowed enclosure called "the picket" where guards are monitoring the activities going on in two adjacent tanks that each hold 50 plus men. There is always at least one guard, sometimes two, men and women. I have categorized these guards into three types: mean spirited, indifferent, and decent. It is interesting to note that women guards tend to be more controlling and even more verbally abusive than the men, often employing exceedingly foul language to bring home their point, warning, or command. "Get your 'f'ing asses lined up for count!" is one example of daily language use amongst them.

Next to the picket on the same far wall there is a bank of 3 telephones which inmates can use to make only "collect" calls; a very expensive "system money maker". Local calls are approximately $4.00 for only fifteen minutes, the usual allowable time frame to talk on each call. The majority of inmates rarely are able to afford such calls, either being completely indigent or having families with little or no extra money for such luxury. I am incredibly fortunate in that I have a very large support network from all over the U.S. who has contributed to my family and myself in our time of need.

So far, I have been able to talk to my wife and other family members and friends at least once a day. Contact with the outside world is a lifeline that keeps the spirit hopeful. Many fall prey to despair and depression because they do not have this lifeline.

Next to the bank of telephones, two of which don't even work, there are two steel toilets with lavatories atop them. These toilets are completely in the open. One is used for urinating, the other for ....! Just use your imagination! The splashing from the first toilet creates quite a serious health hazard. We are given a mop and broom a couple times a day and trustees come in 2 times a day to spray disinfectant, however very conservatively. There are hours each day when the filth and germs accumulate. In addition, guards can and do come in unannounced, women and men, and there is absolutely no privacy when one has to "finish" in full view of these guards. It is a de-humanizing experience.

Next to the toilet on the same wall is the shower surrounded by a chest high 5 foot brick wall except for the entrance which is just open. We stretch plastic garbage bags across the opening to secure better privacy; an act that can land one in serious trouble if caught. There are three shower heads, but only one man at a time showers. We form lines, and sometimes disputes arise over who is next for the shower. Again, guards will come in unannounced and survey us even while in the shower.

The major issue I have with all the restrictions is that 90% of the inmates here are awaiting court appearances and/or trial and haven't yet even been found guilty. Again, the idea of innocent until PROVEN guilty is a thing of the past. Some men have been awaiting trial or appeals from anywhere between 1-3 years. We are all treated as if we are animals who have no rights! Even so, I know that mine is a success story and that I will be exonerated eventually, hopefully while I still live in this world. I have chosen to live with dignity, faith and hope regardless of these circumstances. Actually, my faith in and love for God has deepened while in here and my soul is moved by the illegitimate suffering I see on a daily basis.

In the mid section of the day room, there are steel tables with steel benches (like picnic tables) bolted to the floor where we can sit and write or read, play chess, dominoes or checkers. I prefer to stay in my cell and read or write while sitting in my bunk which is where I am right now. It is slightly more private, not much, but better for me than being out in the open area. There is a television in the day room mounted high up on the wall above our row of cells. Men can sit at the tables and "try" to watch and hear the television. It stays turned on nonstop every day, all day from 8 a.m. until rack down time when they lock us back in our cells for the night. On weekend nights, the day room is open and the television stays on until midnight. The constant drone of the television which is turned up very loud, plus the constant conversation and use of foul language among the men and the slamming and shaking of the dominoes can be quite an assault on the body and mind. It took months for me to acclimate myself to these surroundings.

For some time, it seemed as if the sound had infiltrated my psyche and it was inside me. But just as of late, I have learned to tolerate it. I have even decided that my skills of concentration and focus have majorly intensified. There is one man who makes earplugs out of the bottom of the rubber sandals we get, by cutting chunks and shaping them with an emery board. They are somewhat effective, but unfortunately not noise proof.

We each have two pair of underwear and one towel to last us while laundry is changed out twice a week. Most men will wash out their underwear when showering which is against the rules, and this gives them the ability to change every day. It is a big no-no to hang these on the bars to dry, but the men have found ways around that. We make string lines out of plastic bags by stretching and twisting them and these are hung in hidden places within each cell to hang our towels and underwear on to dry.

Occasionally, usually once a month, there is what's called a "shake down". Without warning, we are told to pack up all our belongings in our plastic bag including our sheet and bedspread and we carry all of this to the gym or into a long hallway. We are then told to empty our bag onto our bedspread and a whole team of guards searches our belongings for contraband. There are really ingenious inventions by inmates to hide things such as "free world" writing pens. A plastic bottle of VO5 moisturizer, which can be purchased at commissary, when it is half empty, can become a holder for these pens. A plastic two-piece toothbrush container fits down inside the bottle. The holder is sealed by plastic and adhesive that has been removed from other containers and is used to keep the pens dry from the remaining moisturizer. Plastic bags are also used, stretched and twisted to make a strong thread for sewing up tears in the rubber sandals.

During the "shake down", once all contraband that they can find is confiscated, we have to strip down all the way and shake our clothes so they can see if there is any contraband hidden in them. At the same time, other guards are searching our cells, cutting down the remaining clothes lines, searching under the bunks etc, etc. On occasion, we are told just to have a seat in the day room while guards search through our bags and bunk areas without us present. For those who have not yet received final convictions, this practice is a violation of civil rights, an illegal search if the person is not present to watch. There are no serious consequences from these searches when harmless contraband like the clothes-lines, food saved up, or extra towels, sheets, boxers, and etc. are confiscated. Sometimes however, tobacco or drugs from the streets make it in and these are very serious. Cigarettes can sell for as much as $5.00 each. One cigarette can be broken down into three and sold for $3.00 each. Inmates have figured out how to short an electric socket creating a spark to catch paper on fire and light the tobacco. Tobacco and street drugs or other serious contraband such as weapons are brought in by corrupt guards or even medical staff. There is an elaborate economic system going on within the confines of the jail.

I can say one good thing about being in here. It can be an intense time of spiritual growth if one chooses to use the time for such. There are prayer circles every night at 9:00 p.m that are held within our tank. A scripture from the bible is read and discussed and then we hold hands, recite the Lord's Prayer and embrace as brothers. Small groups get together to study and discuss scriptures. I have in the past, when in the outside world as a free man been prone to think to myself "Oh! He waits until he gets in jail to get religion." But now I see it much differently. I think of men who were in the trenches of Vietnam. How many of them suddenly "got" religion. When one's life is on the line, I promise you that the majority will reach for God. Believe me, I am 57 years old, and years of my life have been taken from me thus far through this experience and even more of my future years are threatened. I am one, however, who refuses to cave in to resentment, despair or hatred. My love of God and my fellow man, through getting to know them and understanding their motivations, has only increased. And at the same time, naivety has been dealt its death-blow. I have inventoried my entire life and found how much I need God's love and grace and that His forgiveness for wrongdoing is unending if we seek it, with the only requirement being our willingness to forgive others who have done wrong to us. Jail may not be optional, but spiritual growth is. There are many religious creeds, doctrines, sects etc. and many religions "about" Jesus, but there is only one religion "of" Jesus. If you truly desire to know his religion, seek it within your own heart and mind and you will find it. I may sound "preachy", but there is NOTHING more important than the state of one's soul. Said the master "The Kingdom of Heaven is within you."

FRIENDSHIPS

That first night, when I finally reached my current home away from home, I was terrified. There was no one to explain what one is supposed to do. I imagined I was being put in a large room full of rapists, child molesters, murderers etc. The fear was palpable. That first night, it was well after midnight and the cells were all locked down when I first arrived at the tank where I was to be housed. I took my mattress and found a place in the day room to lie down. The next day I was actually treated with a bit of respect. Anyone who has gray hair is referred to as "old school" and at least some of my fear was lessened. I was invited into one of the cells – "A" cell, and given a top bunk.

That whole first day, a man named David B. who is a 55 year old white male, sort of took me under his wing and taught me some survival skills. David is an educated man who has been in jail for four years only getting to see the sunshine one time in all these years. I believe he is innocent of his charges like me and is incarcerated because of the words of one person. David taught me to ask God for peace. We discuss books, religion, philosophy and many other subjects. I have learned how to survive here primarily from him. He taught me how to say "no" to others, or to trade rather than just giving away my things when someone asks me. Not everyone is as privileged to have some material sustenance as I am. There are those who will try to take advantage of kindness. One must learn to be "gentle as a dove, wise as a serpent". David and I also banter a lot. He has a smile on his face most of the time and is always ready to help someone in reasonable ways. He has spent most of his time learning the intricacies of the law regarding sex related charges and in fact has given his attorneys most of the ammunition to use in his case. His appeal will definitely overturn his conviction. He is fond of saying "They beat us in court and we then win with the law".

Again, as I said before, prosecutors care only about winning, not about the truth. But if one takes the time and has resources, our law as it is written (not practiced) is the very best on the planet, and will in the higher courts have to prevail. And in the event one who is innocent does not prevail, there are even higher courts not of this world where justice does prevail. And in these higher courts mercy always consults justice. David is a man who has lost everything material in this world including his home and all financial resources adding up to nearly $280,000. His employer has recently spent an unknown amount of money on the best appellate attorney in Houston and he is currently awaiting his appeal to be filed. Please, with me, lift him up in your prayers. He is a good human being who has done much to help many who are less educated and less fortunate than himself.

If my narrative seems to go off on tangents, it's just the way it is coming out of me, just as if we were having a conversation at my kitchen table. With that said, I want to introduce you to a few others whom I've been living in close proximity with, meaning just a few feet, for the past nine months. Gene W. is a 48-year-old white male in my cell. He sleeps above David. Gene's case is another travesty of justice. After 15 months in jail, his case finally went to trial and the jury deadlocked and resulted in a mistrial. The court-appointed attorney only visited Gene a couple of times during his incarceration. Whenever a mistrial happens, the prosecutor has to decide whether to re-try the case. The cost for such a trial is close to $30,000.00. Prosecutors and judges are hesitant to re-try cases that have ended in deadlock. Nevertheless, the prosecutor has offered Gene a small sentence instead of a new trial. When he refused, they came back with reducing the charge to a misdemeanor. The pressures of jail can weigh heavily on a man to the point where he might be willing to accept an offer like this, even when he is innocent. The other choice a man has is to wait for a new trial or a dismissal. Prosecutors rarely dismiss cases. They prefer to set a man off, (in Gene's case it would be next year, 2009) making him wait so long that he would eventually cave in from the pressure and accept a plea deal. Convictions are ALL they are interested in!! Gene does his best to stay positive. He goes to the gym for exercise three times a week. He keeps a record of what he does; so far, close to 5000 push-ups as of the date of this writing October 2, 2008.

Phillip sleeps above me. He is a 57-year-old black male that keeps a constant good attitude. He is a very spiritual man who shares and lifts the spirits of those around him with his smile and whistling and with his refusal to get into conflict or to allow this experience to bring him despair. Again, this is an example of our broken system where a man who is innocent has been sitting behind bars in jail for three years, seeing the sun only one time within those three years. Inmates are thrown away behind closed steel doors and bars, dehumanized and then railroaded in this system of so-called justice.

There are those also who are guilty of their crimes, but even these do not receive the impartial "innocent until PROVEN guilty" treatment, and when they are convicted, they are also thrown away. Many of these men could receive treatments that have been proven effective. Our punitive system is still stuck in the Dark Age of evolution and our technology has surpassed our humanity.

The prison industry in Texas is one of the fastest growing industries. You can research the statistics online. Again, most people are asleep and need to wake up to what our country is becoming. Our priorities are in many instances wrong. We should have spiritual and religious priorities in the foreground and economic and political priorities in the background. The real solutions to all of our problems are spiritual solutions.

We have a law library here at the jail and we are granted one hour a week to study and try to understand our case. For those who don't have paid "free world" counsel, which is the case with most, there is little chance that their level of education can even begin to fathom the complexities of law. Court appointed attorneys as I have seen first-hand, do not fight for their clients. They are primarily interested in staying on the good side of the judges who give them their assignments. They are not paid as well as "free world" attorneys and their effort to defend is in direct proportion to what they are paid. Even so, they do make very good money because of their caseload.

Well over half the population here is African-American with the Hispanic population being the second largest in number; I would venture to say that 75 to 80 percent of each of these groups has court appointed attorneys. In our tank, a man with a court appointed attorney very rarely, if ever, gets a visit from his attorney to discuss his defense. They promise to come at every court appearance which almost always ends up being rescheduled because the prosecutors are not ready.

Speedy trial no longer exists though it is a constitutional right! They make the promise, but almost NEVER follow through with what they say they will do. Men are simply thrown away and kept completely in the dark. Gene, as I said, has had only two visits from his court appointed attorney in 19 months!

THE BEATING/THE PEPPERSPRAY

In terms of violence, the threat of it always stays just below the surface. There is a whole inmate code of conduct unwritten that a person has to learn in order to stay safe. Even then, there are no guarantees. Racial tension can run high during certain times. One never knows when violence will erupt. The fights usually take place in the cells away from the sight of the guards and can be very brutal. This brings me back to my first week here.

I have mentioned that I had been on an anti-depressant and an anxiety medication while awaiting trial and out on bond. I have never needed or wanted this medication before this horrific ordeal made its way into my life. As I was being processed in on that first night, I had informed the authorities of what prescribed medications I had been taking. Because of their lack of concern, I was suddenly deprived of these and within a week started having a horrible detoxification effect. I began to hallucinate. I would see and talk to people who were not there and I would imagine that horrible things were happening to my wife. These were just a couple of the hallucinations I was having due to being suddenly taken off my medication. This began to disturb everyone in my cell because I would stay up all night talking while everyone was trying to sleep. Finally, I had convinced the guards to take me to the clinic. It was interesting that I was fully aware that

I was not being myself. I would go in and out of reality and still recognize doing so.

I told the doctor what had been happening and she gave me a very strong medication to help me come through the detoxification more easily. I assumed they would put me in a different place in order to observe me. When I suddenly realized I was being taken back upstairs where I had been before, I simply said "Wait, I can't go back there. I need help; the inmates are upset with me." Just then, the two officers who were escorting me used the excuse that what I had just stated, and the fact that I had stopped walking meant that I was resisting detention. They threw me to the floor, face down, handcuffed me and dragged me into a nearby room. A third man entered the room and the three officers proceeded to kick me and bang my head several times against the concrete floor. They then sprayed a 50% solution of pepper spray directly into my right eye. It was the most excruciating pain I have ever experienced. They let me scream for a couple of minutes and then slowly walked me to a lavatory where I was able to wash my eye out. I held my eye under the water for about five minutes. The pain subsided, but it was about 45 minutes before it was gone. They then took me to the first floor to be written up and charged with an inmate offense.

Okay, I'm going to interrupt the sequence here to give you an up to the minute account of the events of this past week, the week of October 7, 2008. It has been a very strange week with the type of events happening that I wish I could forget. An eighteen year old man, still a child in my eyes, has been raped at night while locked in his cell. Although, I did not witness it, it was talked about throughout the tank for the next few days following the incident. Of course, the man who did it claimed in the criminal investigation that followed, that it was consensual. We all knew better. There was at least one eye witness, but there are most likely more who are reluctant to say anything. The big fear, of course, is that they might run into the perpetrator later in the prison system and have no protection from the likes of what has happened to the victim, or worse.

The man who committed the violence is a 35 to 40 year old black male who had already spent ½ his life in prison. He is a big man and no one will challenge his physical prowess. He told me when I ran into him later in the gym that he had always had a "punk" in prison and that this victim was just another "punk" who wanted it to happen. I told him that even if that were true, that he was a grown man and that he knew better than what he had done. Because I am an older graying man, for the most part I am able to say what I want. Older men are usually left alone and not harassed, unless they are mentally ill. I also told him that if he were innocent like he claims and even if the courts of this world find him guilty, he will also have the courts of Heaven in which justice is always served. He just dropped his head and said "You shore right." Both he and the young man were moved somewhere else to different tanks.

The second incident which occurred this past week was that of a man who is an MHMRA patient and in the middle of the night he tried to commit suicide by cutting his wrist. He's a man who is always being bullied by others. This man should not even be here. His arms and neck have 15 to 20 scars from previous cuttings. He shared with me that he had witnessed his mother's murder and that he still did not know how to deal with it. He watched as she was shot in the face during a robbery of a convenience store the family owned. Billy worked there. Being uneducated and completely alone in the world, I feel that he doesn't even have a chance. I bring this up to make you aware of the kinds of people that are in here; a mixture of real criminals (the minority), the defenseless who are thrown away by society, and the innocent. I pray for this man often as I know he has a good heart. It is good, but it is full of pain and fear like a child who has been abandoned and is lost in the crowd without a way home. Is this America, the supposed most civilized country on the planet?

The third and last important thing that has happened this week is that my good friend David B. who I spoke about earlier has been transferred to the Texas Department of Corrections. He taught me a lot about how to survive in here and I will miss him. But I am also glad he is gone. He has been in this jail without sunshine or proper food and exercise for four years. His case is a complete travesty of justice. I have lived side by side in close quarters with this man for 11 months now and believe in his innocence with 100% of my heart and soul. He, like me, was convicted without any evidence whatsoever, save the words of the "alleged victim" who changed stories multiple times, creating new ones along the way. In the end, the judge sentenced him to 75 years. He took it with a smile, telling me that he knows with certainty that he will be exonerated in the higher courts. Being college educated, he has spent the last four years in county jail continuing his education in the law library once a week. As mentioned earlier, he knows the laws regarding his particular kind of charge backwards and forwards in addition to his extensive knowledge of court procedures that are almost entirely disregarded by prosecutors and judges alike. I believe him when he says he will win with the law. His case has been appealed and he will never stop fighting for the freedom that has been stolen from him by corruption, power and greed.

SOLITARY CONFINEMENT

After being written up for supposedly resisting detention, I was taken to the clinic again where I was looked over, laughed at by the nurses and other officers who joke about inmate beatings. I was then locked up in solitary confinement. As mentioned, I was detoxifying from the anxiety medications that were abruptly taken from me after I had been taking them for 12 months as prescribed by my doctor and while still free on bond and awaiting trial. The jail doctor had given me some medication that would supposedly help me through the detoxification. However, for the next 24 hours, I suffered severe hallucinations, insomnia, and came very close to a nervous breakdown and retreat from all reality; all this while in a 7x7 foot steel cell with no mattress and no blanket, just a steel bunk, a toilet and a sink. Somehow at some point the next day, I drifted off into unconsciousness and I have no idea how long I slept.

When I awoke, there was a tray of food sitting on an opening in the steel door. Aside from this opening, there was only a small steel reinforced window to look out into an empty day room. I could also see other cells like mine, some with other inmates standing there looking out like me. There was a green mattress on the floor outside my cell with a sheet and bedspread. Eventually, the guards got around to opening my cell so I could get the mattress and covers. They had also gathered my belongings, what was left of them, from my previous home on the fifth floor. This 7x7 foot cell was to be my home for the next 70 plus days.

Within a few days, I was taken to a disciplinary court in which two officers found me guilty after I told them what had happened and I was given a disciplinary punishment of 30 days without visitation or commissary privileges. I remained in solitary confinement for 70 days and after 30 days I was able to begin receiving visits and commissary privileges once again.

ISOLATION OR SOLITUDE – A CHOICE

After a few days, I finally regained my right state of mind from the detoxification. The medications my doctor had prescribed were Zanax and Prozac considering I was under tremendous stress while on bond and awaiting trial. If I had been slowly taken off these seriously addictive drugs by my caring doctor, I would not have suffered the horrors of the abrupt removal of them from my nervous system. I had no idea of the danger of taking these chemicals or being taken off of them when not under a doctor's supervision or care. The lack of consideration given and the indifference of the medical staff of this county jail are absolutely appalling!

I made some decisions after much prayer and reflection that I would see the time I had to do in solitary confinement as a monastic experience. Over the next 70 days, I read the entire Bible cover to cover save for skimming over the "so and so begat so and so" in 1 Chronicles. I developed a routine of some yoga exercises that I had learned with my wife and that she sent to me in the mail. I also read the book by Victor Frankl, Mans Search for Meaning, which is a description of how he survived a Nazi death camp. Reading the literature helped me to put my experience into a larger perspective and I realized that my suffering was small compared to that of Frankls and many others such as Job or even Christ.

While in solitary, I reflected on my entire life going back into every nook and cranny that I could remember which held significance. It was an enormous time of growth for me spiritually and mentally. The 7x7 cells opened into a day room which consisted of a shower and phones. I was allowed one hour each day to go out of my cell to make a call and shower. The fact that I have a loving wife was and is a great solace for me. I called her when I could and those 15 minute calls to her kept me connected to the world. Letters from friends and family continued to come in the mail and I would spend my time thoughtfully answering them.

After a while, I got to know the other inmates in solitary. While out for the hour per day, we were allowed to go to another's cell and talk through the meal slot in the solid steel door. I found that most of the inmates there were without resources and/or support of any kind. I met men who were convicted killers, drug addicts, men charged with sex crimes and probation violation. The interesting thing is that these men are human beings and they have souls that long for God. I am in no way whatsoever condoning their crimes, but I wanted to offer a broader perspective for you to consider. These men mostly responded well to me as I tried to uplift them and teach them. I created a poetry contest after about 30 days and I had five or six men that entered. I gave Ramen Noodle soup as the prize for the best poem. The depth of longing and pain and guilt and even the hope of redemption that emerged from these men astonished me.

This particular "solitary confinement" cell block housed about sixteen men. It had two floors with a stair leading up in the middle of the day room to the second floor. The guards looked out of an enclosed room on the second floor where they were able to see all sixteen cells. I witnessed several attempted suicides there, one of which was a hanging. One of the inmates, while on his hour out, brought his bedspread out of his cell and while guards weren't watching tied the bedspread to the stair landing leading up to the second floor and the other end around his neck. He was hanging there for all to see. When the guards noticed amid all the yelling, they came running and were able to free him from the makeshift noose. Others attempted cutting veins in the arm or neck. It is hard to say whether these men were seriously trying to kill themselves, but they obviously were under tremendous pressure to commit these acts. One inmate during my time there went out of his mind and started throwing his feces out into the day room. This is the world I lived in for over seventy days.

When my visitation privileges were restored, I was handcuffed behind my back and shackled at the feet before going to the visit and had to stay that way for the duration. It was humiliating, but I learned to look at it with joy most of the time. The reason for this is because my wife and friends were ever there for me and provided a link to the outside world which many do not have. There were also periods of deep feelings of loneliness and despair that I went through while in solitary. During these grieving periods, all I could do was weep. But something inside me also knew that there would somehow be an end to the tears. The lessons I received in my years of recovery from alcoholism had given me the ability to know and allow myself to feel and to express my emotion during these normal periods of depression and grief.

During this time, I began to learn the value of solitude. My relationship with God as I then understood him began to deepen. There were periods of inner peace and even joy in the midst of all this conflict that even now continue to grow inside my soul. I am writing this narrative today on October 19, 2008. The solitary confinement experience happened toward the end of December 2007, ran through Christmas and the New Year and in early March 2008, I was finally released from the confinement of that 7x7 ft. steel cell and moved back to the fifth floor and I remain here still today.

THE APPEAL

I realize that this narrative jumps around in periods of time quite a bit and that you, the reader, may get somewhat confused. It just cannot be helped. I am not a professional writer, but I am doing the best I can, writing from my heart, to give you a true and accurate depiction of my experiences in here up to now.

After the trial court announced the guilty verdict, my attorney immediately filed a motion of "Prose Notice of Appeal". This occurred on December 19, 2007, and at the same time a "Motion for a New Trial" was also filed. Because my case was heard by a visiting judge from Austin, we hoped that when the actual judge of my particular court reviewed the errors that occurred during the trial, that he would grant a new trial. He denied the motion for new trial without reason and by law is not required to give any explanation for his decision. Initially, the actual "appeal briefs" to be filed by my attorney were due 120 days following the date of conviction. That would have been April 15, 2008. For one reason or another, extensions of time became necessary which caused a delay in the time the briefs were to be turned in. The new date became July 15, 2008.

Before we could proceed, a new contract had to be negotiated with my attorney. This was because the original contract only allowed me his representation through the trial phase. My friends and family members who were present during the trial were absolutely shocked at the outcome, but quickly rallied and met with my attorney just a few days after the conviction. My attorney agreed to offer his services for my appeal for $25,000.00. This meant he would represent me at the two state levels of the appeals process, the second level being the highest court within the state of Texas, The Court of Criminal Appeals located in Austin. The first level is a three judge panel located here in Houston. There are two of these panels which are the First and the Fourteenth District Court of Appeals. These three-judge panels are required to write an opinion after reviewing the trial court's decision, as to whether they agree or disagree with the decision. The highest court in Austin is not required to issue and opinion. It is a very complex process and I believe it to be the best in the world; that is if there are men and women of integrity and moral character who will uphold the principles of neutrality in their discretions while reviewing the appeals. I have recently seen stories in the news all across the country about the abuses of power by those holding these "life saving", or "life condemning" positions of trust. Sadly, many of our judges have given in to the enticements of power, lust and greed, rather than upholding the principles of fairness, unbiased discretion and the seeking of the truth. It is apparent from a simple review of history that nations can rise up or fall depending on the adherence to or neglect of these principles.

OUTPOURING OF LOVE

I was broke and had no money left to pursue the appeal. After finding out what the fee to have continued representation was, a few friends, my wife, my sister and my daughter met at my home. After long conversation, they were able to devise a plan to solicit donations from all of my friends and family members, acquaintances and even friends of acquaintances. Unbelievably, within two weeks, $25,000.00 was raised on my behalf, by sending out emails and making phone calls to contacts and whatever else could be done to raise the money. Small and large amounts of money from all over the country began to roll in to the trust that my wife had set up on behalf of my appeal. The attorney had said that he needed the fee before he could begin the appeal process and that we could have two weeks to come up with it in order to pay him. We did it, or I should say they did it!! I was completely overwhelmed with gratitude at the outpouring of support and love for my family and me. As I mentioned earlier, crisis can be a great opportunity for the best within people to emerge. The outcome resulting in the deepening of relationships between friends and family is immeasurable. On the last evening of the two weeks we were given, we were still short by $3,000.00. A dear uncle of mine who I haven't seen in ten or more years came through with this final amount of money. I am truly blessed.

My attorney filed the appeal briefs July 15, 2008 and then an amended version more towards the end of July. Normally, the district attorney would have thirty days from the date of file, to file his response to the appeal. The district attorney's office uses a special appellate attorney to respond. These prosecutors are not even in attendance at the trial, but will only read the transcripts and the defense attorney's appeal briefs in order to formulate their response. As of this date, October 19, 2008, the prosecutor's office has failed to produce any response at all. They have asked for one extension and then another because of Hurricane Ike and the last date they were given to file that I am aware of was October 10, 2008; nine days ago. I am in limbo at the present time just waiting for the district attorney's office to finally file their response.

My attorney based his appeal on seven different grounds that are all preserved errors because of the objections he raised at the points in trial that these errors were made. In the appeal, there are many cases sighted by my attorney where convictions have been overturned on the same grounds that have been filed on my behalf. The nature of our, in principle, "the best on the planet" process of justice is that our laws and their processes of enforcement are subject to the interpretation of men and women. For that reason, there may be as many cases sighted by the District Attorney showing where appeals courts have upheld similar types of cases. Although, I refuse to become pessimistic, I am also aware that I may lose this battle. But I assure you, I will win the war!

TRUE FRIENDS

Before I stop for now, I want to introduce you to two additional men who have helped me tremendously to make my time here "worth it". More important than all that I have learned, more important than even the spiritual growth I have achieved, more important than all the knowledge I have gained, is the simple brotherly love I have rediscovered that has come from chance meetings within horrible conditions. When I think of all the billions of people who have been born, lived and died here on our earth, and all the billions that now live and all the billions yet to be born, what are the odds that I would be alive at the same time and the even greater odds that I would happen across the path of any particular human being that I have ever met? And then to be able to form friendships that have the possibility of becoming real love and to learn this true overriding purpose of being alive.

Friend-ship is a ship that two or more friends take a journey together on, and who knows how long the journey will last? In the end of his life, Jesus Christ called his apostles his true friends. The older we get, the more possible it is to become isolated, but this is always our own choice. In today's world, there is a danger that our technology will surpass our humanity. A touching email from a friend does not even compare to a loving embrace between friends. My two best friends here are Jose and Michael. I met Jose first probably ten or so months ago. He is in his mid thirties, a mountain of a man in more ways than even he knows. He is one of the hungriest men I have ever known; hungry for knowledge, for goodness, for truth and for beauty. He is an artist and is incredibly talented at that. He keeps us all laughing with his caricatures of us and keeps us all crying with love for our families, as he so accurately portrays their likenesses from photos we receive, using only pen or pencil. Like me, he is struggling to find meaning in this experience. His heart is as big as Texas and he is striving to seek God in all his affairs. He is a true friend I will never forget. He received fifteen years and is currently waiting to go to TDC. Although this has been devastating, he refuses to become negative and wants to make his life a precious gift to bestow upon his fellows and ultimately God. I believe in him.

Michael, I met probably three months ago. When he first came in, he too had been beaten twice by other inmates while in the holding tanks and waiting for housing assignment. Michael had never seen the inside of a county jail, and by the time he came to our tank, his fear was quite obvious. He had not slept for a couple of days and his exhaustion was also apparent. Upon seeing a prayer circle forming that evening, he quickly joined in and began a process that is transforming his whole being from the inside out. Michael is extremely intelligent having an IQ of approximately 141. He reads an average of up to two good sized novels in a day's time if he wants to. He reads the more complex novels slowly, making sure he gets it. Although his intellect is off the chart, he also has a genuine desire to know truth, to be fair and even-handed to all that he encounters. He and I have a common dream, along with some others, to build a place of real community. We are building it in our hearts and in our minds now, and with God's help we will make it a reality. I have learned much from him about how to manage my own emotions. He has a kind and generous heart, but keeps his affections guarded, refusing to cast pearls before swine. I will never forget him. He is my brother and my friend.

Jose, Michael and I spend time together sharing our lives. We laugh together, we cry together, we rant and rave together; on a ship, a friend-ship made of hope, faith and love.

January 02, 2009

POP

"Pop" Messer was brought into our cell block in late October. He was shuffling with a cane, looked to be in his seventies, almost completely bald. His left hand was clinched in a fist and his left leg remained unbending as he walked, putting it out front first then following with the right leg bringing it ever to the left leg (never putting his right leg in front). After a day I realized he was unable to care for himself. I was determined to do something to help him, so we made room in our cell, #A, for him to move in. One of the guys gave up his bottom bunk as it was obvious he would not be able to climb up to the top bunk. The same man quickly befriended Pop and started to help him with his food tray, medicine call and would just talk to him in general.

Pop had only a couple of front teeth, all the others were gone, and he practically swallowed his food whole. He would awaken each morning throwing up. In the first week, he lost control of his bowels and we hustled him into the shower to clean him up. It was obvious that Pop had suffered a stroke at some point. I took on the job of helping him bathe in the shower. He would have fallen on the slippery floor without help. When men are using the same shower stall to bathe every day, the scum build-up comes quickly. We are not allowed to keep our own cleaning supplies other than what we have for personal hygiene, so we have to wait for the floor workers to come in and clean. Welcome to 21st century America. The floor workers clean once a day and rarely do a thorough job. But this is a whole other subject.

As I've grown to know Pop, I found that he has a sweet spirit, but also that he is an uneducated man who grew up in the backwoods of Louisiana in severe poverty. After the fifth or sixth grade, he had to help his own father provide food for the family by fishing and squirrel hunting.

It dawned on all of us very quickly that Pop had some form of dementia, possibly the beginnings of Alzheimer's disease. His short-term memory was radically impaired. He did not know exactly where he was, what day it was or even the year. Sometimes he could remember his birthday.

How is it possible that the authorities would put a man unable to care for himself in the custody of other inmates without resources to help him? What kind of evil allows for a human being's dignity, especially a harmless old man like Pop, to be assaulted in such a severe and malicious way? I don't fault any one individual, but an unmonitored system gone rabid from lack of true moral underpinning and principled decision making, not to forget the unwillingness of any individual or group to take responsibility, proceeding with an "it's not my job" mentality. I ask then "whose job is it?" The answer is that it is mine and yours!

Pop knew his family, brothers and children and would often talk of them with fondness and longing. Not one of them ever wrote or came to see him. He often thought he was somewhere that he could just walk outside. He did not understand where he was. He had no money and thus could not purchase any commissary. We all shared with him and gave him sweets and coffee to cheer him up. It is a fact that goodness is contagious. Soon everyone in our cell and some others in the block pitched in to help out. I began to walk every day with him up and down the day room. In no time, I encouraged him to discard his cane and walk beside me. He just needed someone to care enough to pay attention. We did! When I was with him, he would begin to re-train the muscles in his leg to walk in a correct manner, but when left alone, he would quickly revert back to his shuffling walk, although he would do so without his cane.

Through our constant complaints to the guards, he was finally given a wheelchair, or what I would call a broken down excuse for a wheelchair. It was necessary for him to have it on the long trips to the court settings in which nothing ever happened that we know of. He would return each time without paperwork or any memory of what had happened. When we would inquire, the guards just would say that he had been re-set.

Although Pop "seemed" to be making some strides physically, his mental acuity was quickly deteriorating. It is now January 2, 2009. Just after Christmas, Pop got his meds and took and unknown quantity. He should not even have been allowed to keep meds on his person. Prior to the event, I had given him his meds (five different ones) everyday. The only one I recognized was aspirin. It would have been dangerous for me to keep his meds for him. I could have been charged with a crime had they been found in my property.

Pop was sick for a couple of days after the medicine incident. Finally, six of us in our cell wrote statements. I had previously written similar complaints and turned them in to the guards, all to no avail. The statement the six of us wrote detailed Pop's condition and what had been occurring. In addition, just a couple of weeks prior, I had written a letter of official complaint to the American's with Disabilities Act Committee following a procedure directing the letter to the liaison who is supposed to be in charge of inmates with disabilities. I sent the letter to my wife, who copied it and mailed it to the person as per procedure. I have yet to hear a response. I am a property owner, business owner and a tax paying citizen. It is my understanding that our tax dollars pay for such programs to care for people like Pop. I now know that along with the rest of the justice system, this program which presents the altruistic face of America is in reality another ineffective and potentially fatal miscarriage driven by concern for dollars instead of human beings. Again, I don't fault individuals except for their laziness, but I hold responsible a system of evil that has apparently taken on a life of its own beyond the malice of individuals.

As a result of our statements and with the help of the <u>one and only</u> decent guard assigned to us, Pop was called to the clinic and I was called to accompany him, which is unheard of. The doctors seemed oblivious to his condition. He would have had to have been examined by them back in October. They asked him questions like "What day, month or year is it?", "When is your birthday?", "What is wrong with your hand?" and "What is wrong with your leg?" I let them know all that had happened. They said they would be sending him to the hospital for a "head scan". That was three days ago. As I was leaving the clinic to go back upstairs, Pop called out after me from his wheelchair, "I love you". I love you too Pop. His belongings are still here; his mattress, his meds, and his paperwork that tells nothing and a few odds and ends.

I leave it to you, the reader, if you have a mind to, to investigate for yourselves similar claims as mine. They can be found easily in this age of information. Will you help me, at least try, to make a difference?

Pop is just one example, and I and others came to love him through KNOWING him. I have seen others, a blind man, a man with an enormous herniated stomach, and a mentally retarded man with at least two dozen scars from cutting himself. These are the kinds of men that Jesus ministered to and loved. Our beloved America claims to be "one nation, under God…" Ask any lawyer, judge, juror or prosecutor and I would imagine 80% or more would make claim to Christianity as their faith. How can such blatant hypocrisy be allowed to continue?

Are we so soft and comfortable that we forsake truth for these fleeting pleasures? Will we continue to put the care of our lives in the hands of corruption and greed? The seeds of our principled and bold beginnings as a nation are yet alive within each of us.

January 26, 2009

CASE IN POINT

Today an innocent man was released. After two and a half years of his life had been stolen from him, the prosecution finally caved. After DNA tests failed to implicate him, he was repeatedly offered plea bargains. They wanted him to sign for time so they could register a win. Each time he went to court prepared for trial, they would re-set him for SIX months hoping to break him down. He refused to accept any time for a crime he did not commit.

With his permission, what follows is the general course of events as they unfolded over the last two and a half years:

Salvador Guterrez-Martinez was accused of a felony sexual assault of a minor in May, 2006. He was arrested July 13, 2006. After two DNA tests by the prosecution failed to implicate him and in fact proved he was innocent, he was indicted in November or December of 2006.

He was assigned a court appointed attorney and each time he went to court, was offered a plea bargain. His own attorney continued each time to try to get him to sign for an offered amount of time. When he repeatedly refused, he would be set off for six months to wait for his next court date. After multiple settings and repeated refusals, Salvador was asked in his last court appearance, which was three months ago, what he would accept with the implication that if he did not accept "something", he would be set off for another six months. Staying true to his own innocence, he refused again to sign, telling them to go ahead and re-set his case for trial as he had every time before. Today they dropped all the charges. He's going home tonight.

Ironically, in today's (January 26, 2009) Houston Chronicle on the front page, there is an article about jail overcrowding in the Harris County facilities authored by Liz Peterson, a staff writer. At the end of the article on page A-4, Ms. Peterson records Mark Bennet, a local defense attorney as having said "A lot of people plead guilty just to get out of jail quickly, including some who are probably innocent."

I have been observing these same prosecutorial and in most cases court appointed defense tactics for over a year now. There are a number of inmates in my particular "tank" as it's called who have been here anywhere from six months to THREE YEARS awaiting trial. I have mentioned this before in this narrative, but it is worthy of repeating. In this "tank" 43 of 57 men (75%) are without resource, have court appointed attorneys who do NOTHING to prepare a real defense, and who according to our United States Constitution are <u>PRESUMED</u> innocent until <u>PROVEN</u> guilty, and this <u>BEYOND A REASONABLE DOUBT</u>. I can tell you by personal experience, we are not presumed innocent. We are treated as criminals are in third world countries, as guilty until proven innocent. And this straying from the very foundations upon which America was built has happened right under our eyes while we have been enjoying color tv, air conditioning and Jack Daniels; while we have become walking zombies under the direction of a corrupt and broken justice system. I do not accuse all Americans individually, but a collective apathy arising from self interest in place of unselfish service, greed in place of simple graciousness, fear in place of courage and division in place of unity of purpose.

This collective consciousness seems to have taken a life of its own, existing above and beyond the malice of individuals—in short, a system of evil. But I do not ascribe to a cause arising from outside our control. The so called "Devil" is not the source of this. The source is to be found within each of us and when multiplied by sheer numbers, takes on momentum. And again, this is not with malicious intent that most of us have caused and/or allowed a system in which our priorities are just wrong.

"With Liberty and Justice for All" does not mean the pursuit of power, financial gain or pleasure at any cost. It means we MUST take into account how our decisions affect those around us, and in a shrinking world, those afar, and mostly, our children's children's children and so on. We must understand that we each are accountable. We claim to be a "nation under God". Does God approve of selfishness, ignorance, greed, hatred, divisiveness among his children? Many of us still claim to be followers of Jesus who said "Love your neighbor as yourself" and who said "love your enemies". Are we following or do we just say it's a good principle? Do we gather on Sundays and quote scriptures to each other or do we follow the living Christ into the destitute neighborhoods? Do we visit the prisoners? Do we care for the strangers? Do we feed the hungry and clothe the naked? Do we seek truth and justice with mercy, or do we sit back each night, worn out by our misguided and selfish pursuits just barely making it in a system we helped create and continue to feed? When will we take back our country? When will we deny self and suffer for what is right? When will we reclaim our superior form of government, not because it is a patriotic action, but because it is a light to the world?

READ THE DECLARATION OF INDEPENDENCE FOR GOD'S SAKE! READ THE UNITED STATES CONSTITUTION FOR GOD'S SAKE! READ YOUR HOLY SCRIPTURES FOR GOD'S SAKE AND THEN DO SOMETHING TO WAKE SOMEONE ELSE UP FROM THE ILLUSION OF SECURITY TO THE WISDOM OF INSECURITY! Following righteousness does not bring comfort to the body but to the soul. Following righteousness is dangerous in a world that still persists in darkness. Following righteousness, following Jesus, requires your WHOLE LIFE, not just your Sunday morning! PLEASE WAKE UP! You may think these to be the ranting and raving of a mad man and you would be correct! I am angry at the deceit, the unfairness, the sin, the evil, the ambiguity, the savage and brutal preying upon the poor, the ignorant and the dispossessed. Did you read my stats? 75% in my tank are just such—poor, ignorant, dispossessed, mentally ill and about 90% who are waiting to go to trial, all treated like animals, INNOCENT UNTIL PROVEN GUILTY!???

A TEMPORARY STOPPING PLACE

I will end this section now that I have calmed down a bit. Please understand; this narrative is a totally spontaneous writing from a jail cell after having observed, studied, and reflected upon events as they happen first hand. I do not have access to court records or to any prosecutor's side of a story or any research data that might be available to me in a civilized and principled society even though incarcerated. I am simply reporting to you what is obvious, what I have observed, and my own subjective outrage, as well as, a didactic appeal to the soul of America. I know that what I say in terms of a solution is true. I know we still have it within each of us to boldly, and if possible, peaceably reclaim our citizenship in this greatest of countries. I also know much of what I say is repetitive, but he who has an ear to hear—let him hear!

I have reached a good place to bring the writings of this on-going experience to a close for now. The questions, "Have I said enough? Will people read this? Did I leave anything out? Will any of it make a difference?" To all of these, the answer is, "I don't know." Even if all of this writing or even going through this experience is in the grand scheme of things, insignificant, it is still most important that I go through it and that I write it down; that I continue to stand on the foundation of truth and cry it out to all who might listen. I owe it to myself and to God and to you to take a stand regardless of the outcome; to run the good race, to fight the good fight with the certainty born of faith that in the end Justice, with its ever present and faithful spouse Mercy, does prevail.

A BATTLE WON (BUT NOT YET THE WAR)

Two days ago on Tuesday, March 31st 2009, my conviction was overturned by a three-judge panel in the 14th District Court of Appeals. The panel, in a unanimous decision reversed the trial courts decision. There had been seven points of error that became the grounds upon which the appeal was filed by my attorney. After agreeing with our position on three of the points, the appellate judges saw no need to address the remaining issues: "Having found reversible error on issues one, three, and six, we need not address appellant's remaining issues. We reverse the trial courts judgment and remand this case for a new trial." This was a glorious Victory for my eyes to behold indeed!

This just goes to validate all I have said about the lack of interest in the Truth (at the trial level) and the use of (go to any length for the win) tactics used by the so called trusted servants of the Judicial System for the purpose of aggrandizement, money, and ego inflation all rooted in pure selfishness and evil.

From a worldly perspective, the only reason I have gained this partial (as of yet) victory is because I am a man of some, though limited, financial resource with unbounded support from family, church, and literally hundreds of friends, business colleagues and even acquaintances who believe in me. When I say I am a man of resource, I mean I was able to secure what I have always considered to be the very best attorney to represent me, even though it cost my wife and me every cent we had, over $60,000.00, and every cent that was donated, over $25,000.00. There are thousands sitting in jails **FALSELY ACCUSED** with no resources, little support and who are beset by a lack of education (a major factor) that leads to despair, hopelessness and defeat.

The system of so called justice is a mockery of all that is decent, fair, American, and godly. Preying upon the population of ignorance and poverty and using a body of law that is akin to the Salem Witch Hunts, the prosecutors can and do use the words of one person against the words of another to send human beings to prison, sometimes for the rest of their lives. I recently watched helplessly as a 19 year old young man who had a 16 year old girlfriend was sent to prison. And on top of that, this "boy" (not yet a man because our current culture does not foster true manhood) has to register for the rest of his life as a SEX OFFENDER. I lived in close proximity with this boy/man and I promise you in front of God that he is not a sex offender. I am outraged by this. For GODS SAKE, LET US WAKE UP.

Go to Allen Cowlings website: allencowling.com and see the truth for yourself. Don't just dismiss this or choose not to even look. This is your America, your children's and theirs and on and on. If you are uncomfortable reading this, GOOD. We are a spoiled and lazy people when it comes to involvement in our political destiny. Our pursuit of our own goals and dreams at the cost of our values and highest meanings is an assault upon everything our country says it stands for. I do not attack individuals, but rather I am ruthless with the conscious use of evil, pure selfishness, hidden combinations of power, fear, and greed!

Answer this question honestly. How many of you had any idea that you can be charged with a crime, indicted, convicted by a jury of your peers and sent to prison based only upon the words of one other, no evidence at all required? Is this "INNOCENT UNTIL PROVEN GUILTY"? If you are Christian, go right now to Deuteronomy 19:15 then follow it up with 2 Corinthians 13:1. There you will find principles upon which the Truth of a thing can be established according to God! I am not talking of religiosity, or following the dictates of men and women who were "supposed" to have lived 2000-4000+ years ago. I am appealing to common sense, the intelligent use of Reason governed by principles grounded in moral truth which is obvious to any minimally educated citizen of planet earth.

So even if your persuasion is not Christian, no one can argue successfully against TRUTH and stand long. One who attempts such becomes a house divided and will crumble in time, EVERYTIME.

America was founded upon the very highest principles that can be known to mortal mankind: Representative Government, Religious Freedom, Civil Liberty and Unity of Purpose as One Nation under God with Liberty and Justice for All, and that means whatever you understand God to be. I may be repeating myself and will probably repeat myself again and again because I believe in what I am saying and have thought it through from every possible angle available to this particular personality over the last 16 months of incarceration. I will go to my grave in an effort to uphold right principles and truth.

APRIL 29TH, 2009

My ordeal, though having ended in triumph in the world of thought and faith is not yet over in the world of physical reality. After the three-judge panel reversed the trial court's conviction, I assumed I would be given an appeal bond. It has now been 30 days since that ruling on March 31st and I am still here.

I have said before that the complexity of traversing the processes of the judicial system broken as it is creates an emotional rollercoaster ride particularly for one who is innocent. The length which prosecutors will go to avoid admitting defeat is a pitiful example of grown men and women, supposed servants protecting our welfare and our freedoms, acting in childish and irresponsible ways. I will relate the month's events in this on going battle for freedom and perhaps you will see through my eyes the truth of this childish yet dangerous misuse of power.

Initially, I thought it was a simple matter for the original court to set a bond and I would be released. This assumption was a misunderstanding on my part of my attorney's consultation. It has only been in the last few days that I learned the intricacies of the process as it has actually unfolded.

Here are the facts: once the appellate court reversed my conviction, the state then had two weeks to file a "Motion for Rehearing". The deadline for filing this motion was to be the 15th of April. The prosecution elected not to file this motion and according to Appellate Procedures, I was "eligible" for release the following day (16th). My attorney filed the Motion for Bond on the morning of the 16th and it was filed in the Fourteenth Court of Appeals here in Houston, (not the original trial court but the same court that reversed my conviction). He asked for a $10,000.00 bond citing my financial situation due to being incarcerated so long. He was also required to give information such as length of residence in Houston, home ownership, employment status, family and community support, etc. He was very thorough and was required to sign his name attesting to the truthfulness of his statements.

Upon receipt of the motion, the appellate judge on the next day (17th) unexpectedly gave the prosecution one week until the 24th to respond to the motion for bond. The 24th came and went with my wife and I on pins and needles, not sleeping well, not eating right, living in a constant state of anxiety simply due to the absence of facts. There was no evidence of a response by the prosecutors which would have shown up immediately on a court Internet website that my wife monitored. My attorney was as dumbfounded as we were and just said we had to wait for the judge to respond to the motion. The weekend was terribly difficult. Then Monday came and we learned that the same appellate prosecutor, who fought for the state in the appeal and lost, filed a late response on the 24th that was accepted by the appellate judge. A copy of this prosecution response was then mailed to my attorney (snail mail) who received it late on Monday the 27th.

The prosecutor stated that he wanted the court to set a $60,000.00 bond, a far cry from the $10,000.00 bond we had requested. His reasoning was that I would be a flight risk because of my age. He stated that he believed I was afraid of dying in prison and that I would probably run if released. He further told the court that I could not possibly have the same support from family and community that I had in the beginning of my case. The truth is that I have even more support now than I had in the beginning. He went on to state that he absolutely would be filing a Petition for Discretionary Review with the Texas Supreme Court. The Petition is due today because the Appellate Procedures allows for the State to file such petition but it must be received by the court no later than 30 days following the conviction reversal. The prosecutor went on to state that should the State be denied the review by the Texas Court of Criminal Appeals in Austin that the prosecution definitely had the intention of re-trying the case in the original trial court. My question to everyone is: **IS THE PROSCECUTOR REQUIRED TO ATTEST BY SIGNATURE TO THE TRUTHFULNESS OF HIS STATEMENTS ON THE REPSONSE TO THE MOTION FOR BOND?** I do not yet have this answer but the question is very important to ask because of the issue of Civil Rights as protected by the U. S. Constitution. My attorney attempted to console me by stating that all these statements are typical prosecutorial conduct, and that the prosecutor is mad because he lost. IS THIS AN ADULT I am dealing with?

He said that the current prosecutor in the trial court has not even looked at the case. The truth is they will have a very difficult time running me through their Kangaroo Court a second time using the same tactics involving pure character assassination formulated from interpretation of events which had happened over 40 years ago. The Appeals Court had already ruled all of that "supposed evidence" that the trial court allowed after defense objection was and is inadmissible and as having no bearing on the charge in my case whatsoever.

Nevertheless, the prosecutors plan is to make it as difficult as possible, spending taxpayer dollars to try and convict an innocent man, rather than using sane and logical principles based in what used to be the American ideal that a person is INNOCENT UNTIL PROVEN GUILTY. What hogwash! Are you outraged yet? If not, then go ahead and continue to open your wallet to pay the salaries of these supposed governmental *public servants*. It is 8 p.m. now and I just learned through a phone call to my wife that the website shows no change so now we won't know until tomorrow the status of the Petition for Discretionary Review deadline filing.

It is now Saturday, May 2nd and the appellate judge has not as of yet acted on the Motion for Bond. We did find out that the State asked for an extension of time to file the Petition for Review. Nothing happens on weekends so now we wait until next week. I have been jerked up then down then up again but now I have reached a different state of mind, hopeful but less excited. The expectations of release carry with them the seeds of disappointment, so in order to stay on an even keel; I must let the expectations go to the best of my ability. I can do this through prayer and meditation and through focusing my attention away from my own troubles and onto those around me. We have had several new men assigned to our tank over the last few days. We had been under a quarantine of our 50 plus man tank for a couple of weeks in April and no one left or came in. It was the result of a case of Shingles or Adult

Chicken Pox found in one of the inmates in our housing, or so we were told.

JEREMY'S STORY

One of these new men has moved into my particular eight man cell bringing our count to nine men. He sleeps on what is called a low rider, a moveable bunk which was placed in one corner of the cell. I want to tell you a bit of his story to draw attention to more of the insanity as it is practiced by authorities in management of this horrendous *Correctional Facility*. Jeremy has lymphoma, the worst kind of cancer. He was diagnosed with it in December of 2008, arrested for possession of four tablets of a drug known as Ecstasy in January of 09. He is 29 years old and the doctors have given him six months to live.

When he was initially incarcerated, he was placed on the sixth floor – a floor designed for the care of those who are moderately ill. After a couple of weeks there, he began to petition the guards to be taken to the doctor because of the increasing intensity of his pain; the cancer was already in an advanced stage. In the Harris County jail, the process of getting to see a doctor involves first seeing a nurse to determine the nature of the complaint or problem. Jeremy claims he was refused a visit with the doctor simply because the nurse did not believe his story of pain. This is alleged to have happened repeatedly until finally when he went to his first court appearance, the judge after taking one look at him issued a court order for him to be taken to a hospital.

After spending a couple of weeks in the hospital and missing a court appearance (the judge assuming he would be back sooner had rescheduled the hearing), he was placed on the sixth floor again then called back to the hospital for a follow up. Over the next month and a half, he was transferred to the hospital a number of times causing him to miss three more court dates. He was receiving chemotherapy treatments and had been placed on the first floor where the more critically ill were placed. At the beginning of April, an abscess began to develop on his neck causing swelling which soon cut off his ability to swallow. After not eating or drinking anything for four days, an ambulance was called and he was taken to the hospital again. The doctor there drained an abscess the size of a softball. They also installed a gravity draining tube to a hole in his neck and he was sent back to jail.

Shortly afterward, there was an incident in which a tray of food during meal time came up missing. The female guard on duty began to search cells. When she came to Jeremy's cell, he was sleeping and completely covered by his bedspread head and all. According to Jeremy, she yanked the bedspread off and in the process ripped the tube from his neck causing a stream of blood and puss to pour out. Again, an ambulance was called and he was taken to the hospital again, where he spent another nine days and was then returned to jail. The swelling was down and he was placed with us in a (non medical) tank. He has a hole in his neck that still drains. We help him change the bandage daily. He is in a wheelchair because of his weakened state. There are no bathing facilities that are appropriate for him here. Do you get this picture? This one man's care has been alleged to have cost the state $2.6 million dollars or perhaps we should call it his lack of care. Today is May 2nd and he will not go to court again until May 27th.

How many more are there like this man in this antiquated house of horrors called a "Correctional Facility"? How long will it take for the people to see and respond to what is happening with outrage or will we all simply choose to ignore it and watch the ridiculously skewed media reports (with a few exceptions) while lounging at home. Or are we so numbed out and medicated with our own poisons that we simply do not care?

May 6th, 2009

THE POETRY CONTEST

When human beings are placed in conditions that test the body, mind and soul to their limits (or what one might think should be the limits), the possibility of a creative response exists. In my own life, I have found writing poetry is among other things, a healthy expression of bottled up emotions, higher values and meanings, the soul crying out to be heard.

I have written poetry for many years and have continued to do so here. One day a couple months back, I decided to have a poetry contest for anyone who wanted to enter. It was on a Thursday and I passed around a sign up sheet with the instructions, some suggested themes and a deadline of Sunday for the entries. There were 15 initially signed up which got whittled down to 12, three having backed out. Being a man of better resource than most (because of my family and community support) I was able to maintain extra commissary items such as Rahmen Noodle soup, pastries, etc. I offered some of these items as 1st, 2nd, and 3rd place prizes. I could feel a stir among these twelve as they went to work over the next couple of days. I want to share these poems, the author's names and who won. I have asked permission to do this from each man and received it. It was a joy and quite an experience for me, and I believe it lifted the spirits of all. I am having the actual hand written sign up sheet and the poems scanned into the computer by my wife to gain a more genuine feel for the reader.

Friend

It was a hot thirst of a day;
When I stop in the corner store,
By the way.

You were cooling in a rootbeer suit;
In rank with others.

We cash in and walk out.

My thirst was gone;
And you hit the ground.

We played kick the can down the street
The ~~is by~~ the way
To treat a friendly drink

Phillip Bowen

Soap Opera Lessons

As sure as the Days of Our Lives,
Some of All of My Children shall
be Young, and The Restless. And if
they don't seek God, either By the
Guiding Light of day or the Edge of Night;
Because they only have One Life to
Live some of All of there days
will end up in Some body's General
Hospital.

My feelings in my heart

I'll hope to see the light instead
but just darkness and void and sadness
I cry out just to be free but locked with
chains and bars If I could pray to the lord
I'm sure he will hear me but I'm afraid of
guilt. I miss my folks and wife like I'll never see
them again. Like a child I cry every nite; what I done;
what they had to do to lock me away forever.

> "TELL THEM THEN"
>
> IF YOU CARE FOR SOMEONE
> IF YOU ENJOY THEIR COMPANY
> IF YOU LOVE SOMEONE
> TELL THEM THEN
> YOU MAY NOT HAVE A CHANCE TO EVER AGAIN
> DON'T WAIT TILL TOMMOROW TOMMOROW'S TOO LATE
> YOU'LL BE DROWNING IN SORROW YOURSELF YOU'LL SURELY HATE
> ONE DAY WILL COME THAT PERSON GONE
> YOU'LL FIND YOURSELF STANDING ALONE
> AND WHEN YOU'RE GROWING GETTING OLD
> YOU'LL WISH YOU'D TOLD THEM A HUNDRED TIMES FOLD...
>
> C. Porter

"TELL THEM THEN"

If you care for someone
If you enjoy their company
If you love someone
Tell them then
You may not have a chance to ever again
Don't wait till tomorrow tomorrow's too late
You'll be drowning in sorrow yourself you'll surely hate
One day will come that person gone
You'll find yourself standing alone
And when you're growing getting old
You'll wish you'd told them a hundred times fold...

Loved,

The heart is like the rose, it need to be cared for, are it never grows. Love is something beautiful and strong. It could be expressed by the way of a song. To be loved is a wonderful thing, so let us be happy from the joy it shall bring, for now the birds sing, wedding bells ring. From you I shall never stray. I promise to love you each and every day.

C Emonit

"Devine Behind"

I Feel down like a clown,
with tears coming down.
I Never thought my heart would fall,
But in her blue eyes I saw.
A beauty like no other true,
What would my life be with you.

If only Love could Flow ~~today~~,
and make you choose to look my way.
Then everyday would feel like autumn,
Cool ~~~~ and crisp with troubles forgotten.
Be mine Bemine O honey devine,
O God of love to me be kind.

By Pedro Martinez

The Good Thing About Today

When I wake up to see that
Today is unlike any other day...

The Good Things about Today

The Comings, The Goings,
The Wondering, The Knowing
The constant shifts of Personalities
Displayed...

I watch I see
I listen I hear I yearn I learn
I Smell I Taste
All sensations I embrace
The Good The Bad
The Sad The Glad
Experiences I encounter every day...
But today is good Because it's
Another day for me to experience
God within a day of Another day...

By Norman Greer

By: Vicente Saldivar

Finding Peace

Here I am again, another night with not much sleep. Laying silently in this cold bed that has no emotions.

Listening to conversations being whispered all around about outcomes, hopes, & wishes desired from everyone. Proves to be the only way to get some relief around here.

Several months here, and its not getting any warmer or closer to bringing fresh air or seeing daylight. Again, I just lay here in bed at night, knowing that I am a prisoner of the Law, hoping to one day be free. Does It emotionally stress me out? Yes! Feels like someone grabs my heart and squeezes until it no longer beats ... making it hard to breath, and even easier for this cruel place to trap and control my emotions.

I have lots of anger inside. I never knew I could hate anything as much as I do this Hell. I want to scream! But instead I lay in bed and listen to other peoples conversations, butting in from time to time for distraction, but only in my mind.

For Comfort I go to GoD & knock on his door to ask the same thing I seem to be repeating more & more each Day:

God please help me, Im in the dark, shine your light on me. so I can find my way home. Take my hand, guide me down the right path".

I know he hears me because it quiets the voice that screams from inside my mind, heart and soul. "Slowly putting me to sleep."

Feels like heaven, so fresh, so soft so pure! "Peace at last". Mentally preparing to start another day, By knocking on God's door, hoping to be the first in line, waiting for him to answer, so I can ask the same ~~thing~~ questions I do every day: "God, please help me, Im in the dark. Shine your light on me so I can find my way home. Take my hand, guide me down the right path",

"I know he hears me!"

"MOTHER"

Mother you may never know the love I
have for you inside, the fact that we can't
spend time together brings my heart so much
pain it's impossible for me to hide.

Offering your life, love, time, and advise
and everything else you have to give,
you risk your all and endure great pain
to make it possible for us to live.

Today is the day I've chosen to say
thanks for the things that you have done,
it takes alot of love, wisdom and strength
for a woman to raise 2 daughters and a son.

Happiness and joy are what you've
given me throughout my days, you've
made my days a little brighter and my loads
a little bit lighter in so many different ways

Emotionaly and spiritualy our hearts will
always be connected, with the care and
compassion that you've shown I feel loved
and never neglected

Realy mom in this whole poem all im
trying to say, is im glad I get to
call you mom and tell you 'Happy Mothers
Day."

Eric Brown

Getting Dressed With God's Armor

I'm strong in You Lord, empowered through my union with You; I draw strength from You, that strength which Your boundless might provides I put on the whole armor which You supply, God, that I may be able to successfully stand up against all the strategies and deceits of the devil. For I wrestle not with flesh and blood, but against the principalities, against the powers, against the master spirits who are the world rulers of this present darkness, against the spirit forces of wickedness in the heavenly spirit sphere. Therefore I put on Your complete armor, God, that I may be able to resist and stand my ground. I stand and hold my ground, having tightened the girdle of truth around my loins, having put on the breastplate of righteousness (integrity, moral rectitude, right-standing with God) and having shod my feet in preparation, promptness, and readiness with the Gospel of Peace. I life up over all the covering shield of faith, upon which I can quench all the flaming missiles of the wicked one I take the helmet of salvation and the sword of the Spirit, which is the Word of God. I pray at all times, on every occasion, in every season, in the

spirit, with all manner of prayer and entreaty. One must keep alert and watch with strong purpose and perseverance, interceding in behalf of all the saints and that freedom of utterance be given me that I may speak boldly the mystery of the Gospel for which I am called.

In Jesus name, Amen!

Mr. H. Smith

I AM CREATOR : Dated, 3, 21, 2009

I'm created In his own beings.
His Love breads ~~~~ Life within
   But, You say I'm Flesh and of
this woeld, however I'm his own beings

I'm created In his own beings
His Love breads Life within
he's created his sights In my being
and has given me thoughts out of
him, however I'm his own beings

I'm created In his own beings
his Love breads Life within
has any one found such as him

for God Is, therefore I. Am
I'm created In his own beings
I'm both woman and man, ho!
did I not mention, I'm Them
Creator of All, You All I Am..

                    C. Harris

The winners were Phillip Bowen, first place with his poem called "Friend". Second place went to Herman Greer with "The Good Thing about Today". Third place was taken by Pedro Martinez with "Devine Behind" and we decided on an honorable mention for Vicente Saldivar with "Finding Peace".

One other man, Michael and I were the judges. On Sunday, we gathered in a circle and the winners were announced and these four men then read their poems to the group. There was clapping, laughter, emotion and general camaraderie among these men lighting up an otherwise dark world if only for a short time.

I have learned how to survive and even in some ways to thrive in this darkness. I have learned that while God does not promise to keep adversity or trial from coming our way, He does promise to walk through it with us holding our hand. He gives us the Peace beyond understanding if we simply ask and receive in faith. The greatest blessing I have known here is learning to lose myself in service to others and I even occasionally succeed in doing so.

LESSONS LEARNED / LEARNING

The lessons have been many and the learning continues. As I near the end of this narrative, for now at least, I want to share the pearls I have gained through the struggle of learning these lessons. I can only claim progress in this most amazing journey of the spirit, mind and body. A friend of mine is fond of saying "Life is rich and full of wonder" and it truly is, rich with everything, pleasures, pains, joys, sorrows, success, defeat and the wonder of it all is that we are made to overcome all of it, to walk in faith and not by sight. After all is said and done, pleasures, pains, joys, sorrows, success and defeat in this world are all temporary experiences and have no lasting substance.

The single most important lesson and one that is of the greatest spiritual as well as material value that I have tapped into is to begin to take an eternal perspective. I can truly say that I am a God knowing man though my knowledge of Him is far from perfect. No longer am I a believer but a knower. To know God is to tap the eternal perspective. To know God is incredibly simple though far from easy. In the same way that it takes a long time spent together for two human beings to truly know one another, we can only know God by spending time with Him, particularly alone time. By spending this time contemplating Him, talking to Him, listening for Him, struggling with Him, crying out to Him, being completely honest with Him, trusting Him, we naturally move out toward those around us in fellowship and in service and we find the gift of self-forgetting. This self-forgetting is the pearl hidden in the closet of meditation and prayer that brings the eternal perspective and the end of fear.

Over the last 17 months, I have been given the opportunity found in crisis to spend quality time alone with God every day. I no longer think in terms of my little plans and designs but in the eternal life of the spirit son of God that I truly am. What is this fleeting 80 or so years but a wink in His eye? There is nothing to fear here or hereafter for one who knows and follows after Him trying to discover and penetrate His heart. He will never refuse the man, woman, or child who is seeking His heart.

Interestingly, this eternal perspective has great practical value. Striving for fearless living, I am much less prone to fall prey to bad decisions, actions, or attitudes that are rooted in selfishness and self-centeredness.

One can begin to place the future completely in God's hands thus freeing one to be fully present in each moment. We can make plans, but not plan results. Decisions and choices are made with more attention paid to how others might be affected. More and more, we want to contribute rather than receive. Our joy becomes full and lasting. We are constantly being born anew and thus we are spiritually alive forever more.

RELEASED

November 16, 2009.

I was released on a $30.000.00 bond on May 8, 2009 and since then I have been rebuilding my life with the new perspectives gained from 17 months of incarceration that I chose to turn into an opportunity for growth.

After the conviction was overturned, the prosecution, upon exhausting all requests for extensions, filed a Petition for Discretionary Review in the Court of Criminal Appeals in Austin. The Petition was filed on June 1, 2009. My attorney also filed a response to accompany the petition to this Texas Supreme Court. On September 16th, the same court issued their response to the Petition. They refused the petition and the case was returned to the 14th Appellate Court. This court then issued a mandate on Sept 23rd stating the appellate process was finished and the case was remanded to the original trial court.

On Friday, November 13th, 2009 I received a call from my attorney who said the 174th Court had set a court date for a hearing. That date is this coming Friday November 20th. Today is Monday and I am preparing myself for this coming date. We do not know what their intentions are and it may be fair to assume that they don't either. We shall see what Friday brings.

February 12, 2010

I have written nothing since the last entry. Life has kept me busy with many changes. Since the November 20th Court hearing which was re-set, there were two additional re-set dates in which we showed up at court only to find they weren't prepared to give a disposition. A disposition, (meaning a decision about whether they would re-try my case in the original court that convicted me), was put off two or three more times in which we suited up, showed up only to find they were unprepared. At one of the hearing dates, the prosecutor told my attorney she could not find my file, but that she knew it was somewhere in the courthouse. She further stated that she had not yet reviewed it (her being a brand new prosecutor assigned to this case) and that she would need time to find the file and review it. Very efficient governing bodies we have here in Harris County.

The next court hearing was set for December 11th and again, they were not ready saying they still needed to talk to the original prosecutor. I was rescheduled again and again. When the original prosecutor was finally contacted by the new prosecutor, we were told he said he wanted to talk with the family of the complainant (that he was very close with them).

Finally the day came, January 14, 2010 when we all showed up for another hearing, this time to (hopefully) get an answer. We were there about a half hour, a whole row of family, friends and supporters who had stayed beside me for the last four years. My attorney approached our group and said "All Charges have been dismissed". A roar went up from that row and we had to be reprimanded for the noise. We took our celebration outside the court and cried and laughed and hugged, and I was overwhelmed with emotion. It was a shock to my system that I was not used to. I wept openly.

That day was January 14, 2010 and the next day, we closed on the sale of our home and have since relocated to the country, a long term vision and common dream of my wife and mine. I took off the armor I have worn for the last four years only to discover a soft underbelly, somewhat wounded but healing. We are surrounded by the woods and their creatures, the stars at night, a sizeable lake full of bass and catfish and the Creator paints a different sunset everyday over the lake. We call this place New Eden.

Who among us knows what is around the next bend in life. I for one feel as though I can survive anything, and I can, for I have gained the eternal perspective. I am a member in the family of God and Jesus of Nazareth has shown me the way to live free regardless of circumstance and I will forever follow Him on this most amazing adventure of life.

To those who read this narrative, I hope you gain something of value, that it in some small way lightens your load or at least makes you know that we all have our loads. Let us help one another with these loads that we might be truly brothers and sisters.

ONGOING REFLECTIONS

August 24, 2010

How can I begin to tell you what I now feel and what I know for certain? I wish there were a way you could see through my eyes, feel what is in my heart. On the surface, my life is a terrible daily-ness. There is an ongoing need to make a living, the seeking of daily bread, an ongoing choice between falling prey to or fending off the onslaught of the television news, the ongoing effort to avoid the cultural addiction to viewing tragedy, misfortune and the second-hand witness of violence, hatred and fear as it plays out in our media streams.

Just below the surface is a living, breathing awareness of my Father in Heaven, His unending Love, His belief in me, and His refusal to give up on me. In a still small voice, He speaks courage to my heart when my spirit is low and brings me down gently when I have flown to lofty heights of arrogance and pride. For He knows my heart, that it is sincere. But I cannot hear this Voice unless I listen. In the closet of my soul, He guides me to seek for Goodness in all things, to find that which is right about life, to proclaim the elements of good praise and high character in my family, friends, and in those who are strangers. He wants me to nurture these qualities in myself and in those who I find in my path. He has taught me and is teaching me to be patient, kind and tolerant, to refrain from holding anger, from over much self concern, from worry about anything at all. I am learning the fine art of self-forgetting and the discipline of any fine art is an on-going achievement. There is no final destination. This is an eternal adventure awakening in me each moment and it is forever the first step on a new path, the letting go of things known, so that I might learn anew. In Romans 12:2 Paul teaches: "Do not conform any longer to the pattern of this world, but be transformed by the renewing of your mind. Then you will be able to test and approve what God's will is—his good, pleasing and perfect will."

He commands me to become as a child, to trust without condition. I am in His safekeeping and even if life tears me to shreds, I have nothing to fear for He is ever with me. He has shown the path to life, and it is the path of following after Jesus. The life of Jesus is not an example to me but a Holy Inspiration, ever calling me to stretch beyond my own limits, to seek the will of the Father for me personally.

I am to comfort the afflicted at every turn, and the light that I shine forth will forever afflict the over-comfortable. To walk in faith is to walk courageously, to uphold what is correct, right and true at all costs, and to confront deliberate wrongdoing in wisdom and meekness. Ah, but wisdom may sometimes seem foolish to the eyes of the world because it demands an end of mediocrity and status quo! And meekness is boldness because it is dependent on the greatest force in the Universe for sustenance, direction, and instruction. This force is not an outer physical force but a spiritual one and it is found within the secret chamber in the deepest recesses of the heart and mind. If we could but heed the words "Be still"!

I will continue down this path with an abundance of Hope, a certainty of His presence in even the slightest of detail. The lessons of space and time have only just begun. "Do not be afraid" says the Angel at every appearance.

The yoke of the Gospel of Jesus is easy, and the burden of Truth is light. What does this mean? To me, it has meanings on several levels. I think of the word "yoke" and I think of oxen that are bound together giving them the ability to pull a much greater load than the sum total of what they could pull individually. Well, our Lord was yoked with His Father, and in fact on many occasions said that it is "....the Father who doeth the work", thus making the burden light. Another way I think of this is that He was saying that it is easy to do Good. And it is! Many people are heavily burdened by a wrong idea that being a Christian is hard. Why? How hard is it really to do good works? How hard is it to smile?

I know that we too can yoke with the Father through our Lord and that our burdens can be as nothing, even as we carry them. We can find strength we were not aware of within our own being simply by asking with a sincere heart. This is the crux of the matter. Sincerity of heart is the key and how many of us do not sincerely want to be happy, joyous, and free. To be sincere in heart is not adherence to some superstitious set of rules, doctrines and dogma that keep us forever separated from one another. I have heard it said that tradition is the living faith of dead people, and that traditionalism is the dead faith of living people.

Let us sink into our own deepest longings and desires as we let go of pettiness and embrace the differences. I have also heard it said that there are 400 species of wasp in the rainforest and that it takes them all to make up the ecology of the rainforest. In other words, the differences hold the solution, not the problem. Let it be known that we are all brothers and sisters and that we all have one Father, one source, that we are family. Is there any one who would not want to help a member of his own family? There actually may be a few who claim that they would not, but I have seen past these ego defense mechanisms and can testify that Love always has the final say and by asking, the hardest of hearts can be softened. It is interesting to note that at the time of physical death, it is our family that we want close to us.

Let us take great care to maintain a softness of heart that lets God out in public. By trying to hold bitterness, we trap

God inside and our light remains hidden. Ah, but He is patient and suffers long with us, waiting for our knees to bend, for our hearts to open that He might be free to lead us. His love has no end and He will walk with us all the way even down wrong pathways ever seeking that which is lost. When we turn to Him, He finds us and sets us back on the path that is right and good and that leads out of darkness and fear and into the light of faith and love regardless of what trials we face.

RESOURCES

Many in the world especially in the United States live in a world of technology where information is at our fingertips. With the internet, we can access all the resources that are available to us for almost anything we need help with.

There is a growing movement in the United States to confront and change the policies and procedures that can result in wrong convictions and the resulting horrendous damage to innocent lives, families, children all the way in some cases to the execution chambers. This movement includes the examination of the use of illegal and even immoral practices to win at any costs.

Our adversarial system of justice is in grave need of reform and there are many who are working to see these reforms come to fruition. We can see the evidence of these efforts daily in the news with men and women being freed after spending years in prisons and jails. There is much work to do yet to deal with the causes of wrongful convictions.

I want to offer only a couple of resources here that will be helpful to those who are in the midst of fighting for their freedoms, who have been falsely accused, misrepresented, wrongfully convicted, whether you are on bond and fighting or in a jail cell somewhere crying out to be heard.

FALSELY ACCUSED / NEED DEFENSE

Please understand that my recommendation of the following resources is based solely on help I personally received through my own research of these organizations. Whether they will be helpful to anyone else, I cannot offer any guarantees.

Neal Davis Law Firm, PLLC
Commercial Bank Building
917 Franklin Street, Suite 600
Houston, Texas 77002
Telephone: (713) 227-4444
Facsimile: (800) 760-7140
www.nealdavislaw.com

Allen N. Cowling
Professional Investigator
Trial Consultant - Criminal Defense Strategist
Cowling Investigations, Inc.
1019 Ridgeside Drive
Brandon, Mississippi 39042
We Gladly Accept Cases Worldwide
http://www.allencowling.com/

CLAIMS OF INNOCENCE AND WRONGFUL IMPRISONMENT

THE **INNOCENCE** NETWORK

Freeing the innocent and preventing wrongful convictions worldwide

http://www.innocencenetwork.org/

The Innocence Network is an affiliation of organizations dedicated to providing pro bono legal and investigative services to individuals seeking to prove innocence of crimes for which they have been convicted and working to redress the causes of wrongful convictions.

We invite you to use this site as a resource for amicus briefs on post-conviction innocence claims and to learn more about our members, our annual conference and our membership guidelines.

In 2010, the work of Innocence Network member organizations led to the exoneration of 29 people around the world, who served a combined 426 years behind bars for crimes they didn't commit. Read a report on the exonerations of 2010 here.

For news and scholarly articles on wrongful convictions and reforms to address them, visit the Actual Innocence Awareness database, maintained by the University of Texas School of Law.

The Innocence Network is currently accepting nominations for two new annual awards - the Champion of Justice Award and the Journalism Award. Nominations are due by January 8, 2010. Learn more.

The Innocence Network recognizes the fact that in working to prove the innocence of the wrongfully convicted, victims and family and friends of victims are often affected, which may cause legitimate concerns and fears. The Innocence Network has adopted a Statement Concerning Victims which addresses those concerns.

Innocence Project
40 Worth St., Suite 701
New York, NY 10013
info@innocenceproject.org
212.364.5340
http://www.innocenceproject.org/

AUTHOR BIO

Wayland Matthew Fox is a native Texan, married, with 3 children, 2 grandchildren and a huge extended family of friends and loved ones across the US. At present he is an independent contractor as a sales agent for a large company. He has spent much of the last 25 years exploring and speaking out about the issues and ramifications of alcoholism, abuse and addiction. Currently living on Lake Livingston, he stays in touch with childhood friends, loves fishing, gardening, writing poetry, tinkering in his garage, a good argument and wants to live forever.

9 781935 909088